The Big Three: The Lives and Legacies of Franklin D. Roosevelt, Winston Churchill and Joseph Stalin

By Charles River Editors

About Charles River Editors

Charles River Editors was founded by Harvard and MIT alumni to provide superior editing and original writing services, with the expertise to create digital content for publishers across a vast range of subject matter. In addition to providing original digital content for third party publishers, Charles River Editors republishes civilization's greatest literary works, bringing them to a new generation via ebooks.

Visit charlesrivereditors.com for more information.

Introduction

Sir Winston Churchill (1874-1965)

"Winston Churchill led the life that many men would love to live. He survived 50 gunfights and drank 20,000 bottles of champagne. [...] And of course, by resisting Hitler, he saved Europe and perhaps the world." – Mark Riebling in "Churchill's Finest Hour".

Was he "the greatest human being ever to occupy 10 Downing Street"[1]? Or a man whose "brilliant but unsound judgement resulted in detrimental consequences for Britain and for the world."[2]? Nearly 50 years after his death, debate still rages over Sir Winston Churchill's contribution to history. Indeed, now that wartime nostalgia has mostly washed away, in Britain in particular the views on Churchill are more divergent than ever.

On one point though, the biographers and historians remain unanimous: Churchill led an astonishing life as a soldier, world statesman, historian and Noble Prize Laureate. When he died at 90 in 1965, one of the most important figures in modern history had left the stage. From

---
[1] Jenkins, p912.
[2] Knight, e-book location 120.

providing some of the 20th century's greatest soundbytes to successfully navigating Great Britain to victory in World War II against great odds, Churchill was at the forefront of global events for decades, becoming one of the most influential Britons in history. In 2002, he was named the Greatest Briton of All Time, and 40 years earlier he was the first person to be made an Honorary Citizen of the United States.

Churchill will forever be most associated with World War II, but his life was far more adventurous and complex than that, and these other aspects of the man are often overlooked and overshadowed. *The Big Three* details Churchill's life and career, while humanizing the young child who was both aristocrat and hellion, and the young man who had to overcome a speech impediment to become one of the 20th century's most dazzling orators. Along with pictures of important people, places, and events in his life, you will learn about Sir Winston Churchill like you never have before, in no time at all.

Joseph Stalin (1878-1953)

"It is time to finish retreating. Not one step back! Such should now be our main slogan." – Joseph Stalin

If Adolf Hitler had not inflicted the devastation of World War II upon Europe, it's quite likely that the West would consider Joseph Stalin (1878-1953) the 20th century's greatest tyrant. A Bolshevik revolutionary who played a crucial role in the Russian Revolution of 1917 and the establishment of the Soviet Union, Stalin was one of the Communist regime's earliest leaders and went about consolidating power after the death of Vladimir Lenin, whose final wishes were that Stalin be removed from his post as General Secretary of the Communist Party and not be given the ability to take power.

Of course, Stalin managed to do just that, modernizing the Soviet Union at a breakneck pace on the backs of millions of poor laborers and prisoners. Before World War II, Stalin consolidated his position by frequently purging party leaders (most famously Leon Trotsky) and Red Army leaders, executing hundreds of thousands of people at the least. In one of history's greatest textbook examples of the idea that the enemy of my enemy is my friend, Stalin's Soviet Union allied with Britain and the United States to defeat Hitler in Europe, with the worst of the war's carnage coming on the eastern front during Germany's invasion of Russia. Nevertheless, the victory in World War II established the Soviet Union as of the world's two superpowers for nearly 50 years, in addition to being the West's Cold War adversary.

By the time Stalin died in 1953, it was written that he "had found Russia working with wooden ploughs and [is] leaving it equipped with atomic piles." Of course, he was reviled in the West, where it was written, "The names of Lenin, Stalin, and Hitler will forever be linked to the tragic course of European history in the first half of the twentieth century." *The Big Three* explores Stalin's life and work before the Bolshevik Revolution, as well as the crucial role he played in establishing the Soviet Union and turning it into a modern superpower. Along with pictures of important people, places, and events, you will learn about Stalin like you never have before, in no time at all.

Franklin D. Roosevelt (1882-1945)

Franklin Delano Roosevelt might be America's greatest 20th century president, but there's no question that he was the most unique. A well-connected relative of Theodore Roosevelt, FDR was groomed for greatness until he was struck down by polio. Nevertheless, he persevered, rising through New York politics to reach the White House just as the country faced its greatest challenge since the Civil War, beginning his presidency with one of the most iconic lines ever spoken during an inaugural address.

For over a decade, President Roosevelt threw everything he had at the Great Depression, and then threw everything the country had at the Axis powers during World War II. Ultimately, he succumbed to illness in the middle of his fourth term, just before the Allies won the war.

The Big Three covers all the well known highlights of Roosevelt's life and presidency, but it also humanizes the nation's longest serving president, covering Roosevelt's family and famous wife, the philosophical shift Roosevelt led the country through with the New Deal, and the tenacious fighter who battled polio and Adolf Hitler. Along the way, you will learn interesting facts about FDR you never knew, including his distant familial relationship with wife Eleanor, and see pictures of the important people and events in Roosevelt's life.

Chapter 1: Winston the Boy

The splendid honey-colored Blenheim Palace in Oxfordshire was gifted to John Churchill, Duke of Marlborough, by a grateful monarch after his decisive victory at Blenheim, in 1704. It continued to serve as the Churchill family seat over several centuries, and it was here, on 30th November 1874, that Winston Leonard Spencer Churchill was born. Despite its prominence and links to the Churchill family, however, the famous estate was never actually Winston's home. His father, Conservative politician Randolph Churchill, was the brother of the current Duke, and it was during a family visit there that his wife Jennie gave birth to their first son several weeks prematurely.

Blenheim Palace

At that time, the Churchills lived in central London, where Randolph was well placed to pursue his career in government. Although Randolph was not the Duke, Winston's immediate family still hailed from and provided a privileged background from the outset, on the margins of the still powerful British aristocracy. Like any typical British aristocrat, young Winston had public (i.e. private) school from an early age, a nanny, and somewhat distant parenting.

Winston would remember little of those early days in London, for in 1877 the family was effectively exiled to Dublin, where Randolph served as Viceroy. To his cost, he had become embroiled in allegations of adultery which touched on the royal family. Prime Minister Gladstone had to get him out of the way in a hurry. Then a minor figure representing the parliamentary constituency of Woodstock, Randolph Churchill would find political success only on his return to London three years later.

Randolph Churchill

It was in Dublin that Winston developed a strong bond with his nanny, Elizabeth Everest, that would last until her death in 1895. His relationships with his parents were more nuanced. Though he admired and always sought to impress his father, Winston's turbulent school days generated tensions that were difficult to resolve. He adored his American mother, but the constraints and formalities of a Victorian upper class childhood meant that he did not see as much of her as he would have wished.

Lady Randolph Churchill

Back in London by 1880, young Winston developed a fascination for toy soldiers, building an impressive collection and ensuring that they were marshaled by regiment and brigade as he set them out on the nursery floor. He now had a baby brother, Jack, with whom he would remain close until Jack's death in 1947. At seven, Winston was sent to boarding school at Ascot. It was here that he began to display the willfulness which would mark him out as a maverick for the rest of his life.

7 year old Winston

Churchill was far from stupid, but he was disinclined to accept instruction without question, and he put little effort into those subjects which did not interest him - notably mathematics. In the rigid British public school system of the time, this attitude inevitably led to conflict and a reputation as a poor student. Repeated beatings did little to deter Winston from speaking his mind: courage and stubbornness would be traits that were to strengthen and recur.

From Ascot he was moved to a school near Brighton, due to his health. Although happier there, Winston did not excel. At 13 he was enrolled at Harrow, then as now one of Britain's most prestigious public schools. He took up fencing, which he enjoyed, and in which he did well. English and History were his strengths, and when he joined the Harrow Rifle Corps (cadet force) his fascination with military matters became evident.

Courage and stubbornness would later become hallmarks of Winston's that were effusively praised, but in a child his age, they were far less appreciated by his parents. A despairing Randolph Churchill, fearful that his eldest son might turn into something of a failure, encouraged the boy to apply for army officer training. It took Winston three attempts to pass the entrance examination for the Royal Military College at Sandhurst; and when he finally did so, it was for the cavalry, rather than the more prestigious infantry. His father wrote to him in stark terms, warning him "if you cannot prevent yourself from leading the idle useless unprofitable life you have led during your schooldays & later months you will become a mere social wastrel[3]".

That letter, the military environment at Sandhurst, or perhaps the boy becoming the man led to a turn-around in Churchill's performance. Applying himself to his studies, he graduated eighth in his class of 150 and took up a commission in the 4th (Queen's Own) Hussars, choosing to stick with the cavalry despite his high marks.

---

[3] Addison, p. 12

Chapter 2: Stalin's Early Years

Stalin's birth house in Gori, Georgia, within the shrine complex built over it in the 1930s. Today it is a museum.

Ioseb Besarionis dze Jughashvili was born the fourth child of Ketevan and Besarion Jughashvili on December 21, 1879. Though his parents were poor peasants living in Gori, Georgia, he was nonetheless pampered and sheltered during his youth, due to the death in infancy of his three older siblings. By the time he was born, his mother was determined not to lose another child to the grim reaper, so she watched his health carefully and made sure he had the best care she and his father, a boot maker, could provide. She even took up washing in order to have more money to provide better food and clothing for her son.

Ketevan

Besarion

   Despite his parents' best efforts, young Joseph suffered health scares in childhood. At the age of seven, Joseph experienced the first major health crisis of his life when he came down with smallpox. Night after night his mother sat by his bedside, bathing his feverish head with cool water and trying to keep him from scratching the virulent pox that covered his little body. While little Joseph did survive the dreaded illness, he was left with permanent scars all over his tiny face. For the rest of his childhood he would be taunted by his young friends with the cruel nickname "pocky." One of the most famous aspects of Stalin's regime was its willingness to doctor photos for political purposes, and that extended to Stalin's personal appearance itself, as he later had photographs altered to make his pockmarks less noticeable. Despite being merely

5'4, Stalin would ensure that he was depicted majestically and appear larger than the "little squirt" President Harry S. Truman would later describe upon meeting him.

In addition to that major health scare, young Joseph had a turbulent first 10 years as a result of his father's failed business. Though they were initially faring well, Besarion became an alcoholic and abused his wife and son. Furthermore, the family moved several times during the first decade of Joseph's life, and the young kid grew up in destitute, tough neighborhoods. Even as a child, Joseph engaged in brawls with other kids, experiences that undoubtedly toughened the man who would later famously state, "Gratitude is a sickness suffered by dogs."

In gratitude for his survival of smallpox, the devoutly Christian Ketevan decided her little boy had to have a religious education. She scrimped, saved and wrangled until she secured him a place in the little school run by their local church in 1888. This enraged Besarion, who wished to have the young kid trained as a cobbler. After one drunken episode in which he assaulted Gori's police chief and smashed the windows of the local tavern, Besarion was ordered to leave town. He did so without his family, leaving Ketevan and Joseph on their own.

While at school, the spoiled little boy had his first experience with order and discipline, including having to speak Russian in the classroom instead of his native Georgian. Nevertheless, he excelled in studies, as well as becoming so accomplished at singing that he often sang at weddings.

Although Joseph was excelling in school, he continued to suffer health problems. By the time he started his schooling, Stalin had suffered an injury to his left arm, brought about possibly by blood poisoning or physical abuse, that left his left arm a couple of inches shorter than his right arm. Though Stalin later gave conflicting accounts of how it happened, it was serious enough to exempt him from military service in World War I.

Then, in 1890, Joseph had his second brush with death when he was run over by a carriage pulled by two large horses. While there was no internal damage, his left arm was severely injured and for a time it seemed he might even lose it. With his mother's careful nursing over a period of months, his arm finally healed, but the care available in their small village was not the same as was available in larger cities, so Joseph was sent to convalesce at Tiflis, which just so happened to be the town Stalin's father had headed to after being ordered out of Gori. As a result, his father all but kidnapped the child and forced him to work as a cobbler, only to have Ketevan and Gori's religious authorities track Joseph down and take him back. After that, Besarion would never associate with Joseph or his mother again.

J.W. STALIN
Foto 1894

Stalin as a teenager

Because he had always been physically weak, Joseph was accustomed to hours of quiet reading and did well at school, earning a scholarship to the exclusive Tiflis Theological Seminary at the age of 16. While there, Joseph joined Messame Dassy, a secret organization committed to promoting independence for Georgia, and there were also young followers of Karl Marx in the group. This proved to be Stalin's first encounter with the revolutionary socialist ideas brewing in Russia at that time. Stalin continued to read all kinds of literature that had been forbidden, from Victor Hugo's novels to socialist revolutionary material, and he persisted even after being caught and punished on several occasions.

Tiflis Orthodox Theological Seminary, circa 1919

By the time he had completed his first year at the school, Stalin had become an avowed atheist. According to one contemporary, upon reading Darwin's *The Origin of Species*, Stalin remarked, "God's not unjust, he doesn't actually exist. We've been deceived. If God existed, he'd have made the world more just... I'll lend you a book and you'll see."

Four years later, at the age of 20, Stalin was expelled from Tiflis for failure to pay his tuition. However, he had already been in trouble with his superiors for flaunting authority and reading prohibited writings. In fact, the real reason for his dismissal may have been that Stalin was already developing his later legendary leadership skills and had been trying to convert some of his fellow students to Marxist socialism. During his school years, he had insisted that his peers refer to him as "Koba", a Robin Hood like protagonist in Alexander Kazbegi's *The Patricide*, and around the time he left school, Stalin discovered some of the early writings of Vladimir Lenin.

Lenin

The young student now wished to become a revolutionary.

Chapter 3: FDR's Early Life, Education and Family, 1882-1909

Birth and Education

Franklin Delano Roosevelt was born on January 30, 1882, in Hyde Park, New York, to James Roosevelt and Sara Ann Delano. Roosevelt never had any full brothers or sisters, and as an only child he was pampered by his very wealthy family. Young Franklin had the privilege of spending many summers in Europe, where he became fluent in French and German, languages that would prove convenient during his Presidency. Roosevelt was a star student, attending the prestigious Groton Preparatory School in Massachusetts.

After Groton, Roosevelt moved on to Harvard. There, he was Editor-in-Chief of the *Harvard Crimson*, and he majored in history and economics. While at the university, Franklin's fifth cousin, Theodore Roosevelt, became President after William McKinley's assassination. Franklin, though a staunch Democrat, cast a rare vote for a Republican when his cousin ran for and won reelection in 1904.

Roosevelt graduated from Harvard in 1903. A year later, he enrolled at Columbia Law School. He did not graduate but nonetheless passed the New York bar.

Young FDR

The Roosevelt Family

Franklin's family wealth afforded him great opportunities. The Roosevelt family was an early Dutch family that helped settle the New Netherlands, the colony founded by Holland but later taken by England and renamed New York. The early Roosevelt family settled in New Amsterdam, today's New York City, and owned significant parts of modern-day Manhattan. The family owned property around Grand Central Station, which even today remains some of the world's most valuable real estate.

Politics was a well-established tradition in the Roosevelt family. Even in the late 1600's the Roosevelts were participating in New Amsterdam politics: one of Franklin's earliest American ancestors, Nicholas Roosevelt, was an alderman in New Amsterdam.

By the 1700's, the Roosevelt family had divided into two separate branches – the Hyde Park and Oyster Bay branches. Franklin was a member of the Hyde Park branch, while his fifth cousin Theodore was a member of the Oyster Bay branch. Franklin's branch produced prominent citizens dating back to before the Revolution, including Isaac Roosevelt, a delegate to the New York State Constitutional Convention, and James Henry Roosevelt, founder of New York's Roosevelt Hospital.

Isaac Roosevelt

Marriage

Oddly, Franklin Roosevelt married another Roosevelt, from the Oyster Bay branch of the family. His wife, Eleanor Roosevelt, was Franklin's fifth cousin once removed, and was Theodore Roosevelt's niece. It wasn't too difficult for Eleanor to get used to her last name after marrying Franklin; Roosevelt was her maiden name.

Eleanor's White House portrait

Naturally, Franklin and Eleanor met at a Roosevelt-related gathering in 1902, a White House reception for then President Theodore Roosevelt. Also a Roosevelt, Eleanor was born into immense wealth like her husband, and her feminist future was apparent from the beginning. In her teens she considered herself ugly and she lacked self-confidence, but she eventually overcame these discomforts and began to consider female aesthetic standards unjust. She attended school in London, and, like her husband, was fluent in French.

When Franklin and Eleanor met, they were two very different characters. Franklin was garrulous and outgoing, while Eleanor was shy and reserved. Regardless, the two quickly hit it off. Though the two had travelled extensively to Europe – a rarity in the early 1900's – their wealth had also left them sheltered. Eleanor, however, was certainly the less narrow of the two, and during the courtship she took Franklin on a tour of New York's poor tenements, an eye-opening experience for the future President. Social justice was first on her mind, and economics was first on Roosevelt's. It was a match made in heaven.

The Roosevelts in 1904

The two were married in March of 1905, with sitting President Roosevelt in attendance. Because both of Eleanor's parents had already died, President Roosevelt had the honor of passing Eleanor off to Franklin at the wedding. For their honey moon, the Roosevelts took a three-month tour of Europe. Upon returning to America, they settled in New York City. Within five years, the couple had four children, with two more to come by 1916. Of the six, five would survive into adulthood – all but Franklin Delano Roosevelt Jr., who died shortly after birth in 1909.

Theodore Roosevelt

Chapter 4: Cornet Winston Churchill and the Army

Churchill in 1895

There was nothing ordinary about Cornet Winston Churchill. His ambitions were already turning towards politics, for which a spell in the army was a useful springboard. He therefore sought action and fame, and was determined to get both. Astute enough to see the value of self-promotion through journalism, he was also developing lavish tastes, for which some supplementary income would not go amiss. The late Victorian period was not short of combat opportunities for a well-connected British officer and would-be journalist, especially one with boundless confidence and a generous measure of cheek. Consequently, Churchill's early career would not be a quiet one.

His first taste of military action was not with the British Army, however. In October 1895, Churchill took leave from his regiment and together with a friend, sailed for New York, en route to Cuba, where the Spanish army was attempting to put down a nationalist rebellion. Though that conflict and the ensuing Spanish-American War that followed were not primary issues for Great Britain, Churchill had been commissioned to report on the conflict for the Daily Graphic.

Once in New York, Winston stayed with Bourke Cockran, a friend of his mother's and a successful politician with a colorful oratory style. Cockran was to leave Churchill with a stronger sense of his American heritage, an even more passionate commitment to a career in government, and an understanding of the power of the political speech.

As a war correspondent, Churchill's courage made him both more effective and more dangerous. Famously, he was first exposed to fire on his 21st birthday. Notwithstanding this he relished his time in Cuba and wrote a series of colorful dispatches. However, tragedy took him back to Britain later that year: his beloved Mrs. Everest lay dying and he rushed to be by her bedside. This was not an end of it, for his father was to follow in January of 1896. Dead at 45, Randolph Churchill had suffered from a debilitating disease which had caused him to make incoherent and ineffectual speeches in Parliament towards the end. Once the darling of the Conservative Party, combining the high offices of Chancellor of the Exchequer and Leader of the Commons, his had been a sad decline.

Randolph's death struck Winston hard. He concluded that the Churchills died young, and so he must apply himself to his own future with even more vigor. During Randolph's life, matters had remained unresolved between them, and Winston may have come to realize and regret that he had not had the time to prove himself to his sternest critic.

Churchill's first foreign posting with the army came in October 1896, when his regiment was sent to Bangalore, India. It was during this period that the young cavalry officer began a period of intensive self-education, shaped and guided from afar by his mother. He plunged into the classics, going a long way to remedy the lack of a university education normally expected of an aspirant to high office. It took courage and application, as sustained intellectual endeavor would not have been common amongst his peers in the regiment. He was also writing prodigiously. The young child who had proven largely uninterested in applying himself to the fullest extent in classes he did not like was now gaining a reputation and capacity for hard work, another important attribute that would come to be acknowledged by friend and foe alike.

Frustrated by his attempt to report on the Greco-Turkish War (which ended before his arrival), back in India he soon persuaded his superiors to send him on attachment to an expeditionary force headed for the North West Frontier Province. Fighting against the Pashtuns, Churchill had to be ordered to abandon a wounded comrade as the tactical situation deteriorated. Later the man was found slashed and mutilated. He would write about the campaign in The Story of the Malakand Field Force (1898) and in a series of increasingly lucrative newspaper articles. Churchill was making a name for himself.

By the following year, in 1898, Churchill received a posting to Egypt and managed to secure a position with Kitchener's expedition to Sudan against the Mahdist army. As before, he was to write copiously about his experiences, and they formed the basis of his two volume history, The River War (1899). The campaign was a success, and Churchill took part in Britain's last major cavalry charge, at Omdurman. It was here that he witnessed unnecessary cruelty on the British side. His compassion in connection with vanquished enemies was another persistent aspect of his psychology.

Now a successful writer and with growing political ambitions, Churchill resigned from the army in 1899. He had been invited to stand for election for the Conservative Party in Oldham, in a by-election which took place during July. Already noted for his effective oratory, Churchill narrowly lost, in an election in which there was a powerful swing towards the Liberal Party. But he had tasted the cut and thrust of democratic politics: he would be back.

Chapter 5: Stalin the Revolutionary

Stalin in the early 1900s

With an incomplete education, Stalin had problems getting work. On the one hand, professional fields were not an option because he had no degree. On the other hand, he felt menial labor was beneath his dignity. Finally, he got a job tutoring children and, later, working as a clerk. These, however, were simply to allow him to eat. His true vocation lay in writing. He soon became a regular contributor to Brdzola Khma Vladimir, a socialist newspaper based out of Georgia.

Stalin made his first serious foray into politics in 1901, when he joined the Social Democratic Labor Party, whose main goal was to overthrow the Tsar through industrial organization and resistance. His activities within the party led to his first arrest in April of 1902, when he was sentenced to 18 months in prison for organizing a strike among the workers of a large factory in Batum, Georgia. Even after his stay in prison, however, his captors were still concerned that he was going to continue to be a problem, so they exiled him to the famed Russian frozen dessert, Siberia.

Not surprisingly, the determined Stalin didn't stay in Siberia long. Shortly after that Congress, Stalin escaped in 1904 and quickly made his way back to Tiflis, where he once again began inciting workers to strike. Upon learning that the Social Democrats had split into two rival factions, Stalin naturally chose the Bolsheviks due to his admiration of Lenin. These activities brought him to the attention of his hero, Vladimir Lenin, who invited him to Tampere, Finland in late 1905 for a conference of Bolshevik leaders. Stalin was duly impressed by the massive gathering of workers and revolutionaries. He was also intrigued by the concept of democratic centralism, a mode of government that Lenin described as "freedom of discussion, unity of action."

Completely committed to Lenin's teachings, Stalin spent the next eight years of his life promoting democratic centralism throughout Russia. Though his efforts got him arrested on four more occasions, he was never held long before escaping. One has to wonder at the ease with which he was able to thwart the efforts of such a supposedly harsh system. Perhaps his jailors were sympathetic to his cause or, more likely, their sympathy was bought by bribes from his fellow political rebels.

It was also in the middle of the decade that Stalin met and married his first wife, Ekaterina "Kato" Svanidze, and they had their first child, a son, in 1907. When she died later that same year of typhus, Stalin lamented at her funeral, "This creature softened my heart of stone. She died and with her died my last warm feelings for humanity." His feelings for her would not stop him from killing several members of his first wife's family during the Great Purge, including her sister Mariko and brother Alexander.

Ekaterina

The first major sign that political change was on the horizon in Russia came during the 1905 Revolution, a disorganized collection of events including everything from a general sense of unease and distraction among the peasants to uprisings within the ranks of the Russian army. By this time the government was truly concerned and implemented several major changes to the

Russian political system. First, they passed laws limiting the power of the Tsar and his successors. They also wrote a new constitution for the country and established a multi-party political system called the State Duma of the Russian Empire. Taking note of the 1905 Revolution, Lenin wrote, "Only the most ignorant people can close their eyes to the bourgeois nature of the democratic revolution which is now taking place. Whoever wants to reach socialism by any other path than that of political democracy will inevitably arrive at conclusions that are absurd and reactionary both in the economic and the political sense."

The 1905 Revolution failed to bring about the desired effect that socialist revolutionaries hoped it would, leading the Bolsheviks to believe that more forceful revolting was a necessity. A few years after the 1905 Revolution, Lenin would write, "Notwithstanding all the differences in the aims and tasks of the Russian revolution, compared with the French revolution of 1871, the Russian proletariat had to resort to the same method of struggle as that first used by the Paris Commune — civil war. Mindful of the lessons of the Commune, it knew that the proletariat should not ignore peaceful methods of struggle — they serve its ordinary, day-to-day interests, they are necessary in periods of preparation for revolution — but it must never forget that in certain conditions the class struggle assumes the form of armed conflict and civil war; there are times when the interests of the proletariat call for ruthless extermination of its enemies in open armed clashes."

1911 found Stalin living in St. Petersburg, where he soon became the editor of the new magazine, Pravda ("truth"). By now, in closer conformance with the goals of the Bolsheviks, Stalin had mostly dropped his focus on Georgian independence and revolution, partly because the area was dominated by Mensheviks. Though he would always retain his thick Georgian accent, Stalin finally began writing predominantly in Russian.

For the next year, Stalin would be part of the weekly paper, published legally at that time. Still, the government always kept a close eye on their articles and censored anything they did not like. In order to try to avoid censorship, the staff constantly renamed the paper, giving it a total eight different title in two years.

Unfortunately for Stalin, one of his fellow editors, Miron Chernomazov, was actually an undercover agent with the Russian police. His reports to his superiors led to Stalin's arrest in March of 1913 and subsequent exile for life to Siberia. As a result, he was out of the country for the most pivotal events of Russian Communist history, the capture and execution of Nicholas II and his family. How much the tales of this blood-bathed coup influenced Stalin's future crimes against humanity is unclear. However, the event did set the tone for how Russian leadership would deal with enemies of the state for the rest of the 20th century.

A government card from a file used to keep tabs on Stalin

Chapter 6: Churchill and Roosevelt: Ascendant Politicians

Churchill Gets His Start

War with the Boer republics was declared in October. Churchill quickly secured a contract with the Morning Post and began a series of adventures in the country which might have been scripted for the movies[4]. Within weeks of his arrival, an armored train he was traveling in was ambushed by Boer raiders. Churchill, without any military authority, rallied the shaken defenders and organized a defense. Notwithstanding this, Boer numbers prevailed, and he was taken prisoner. Undeterred, Churchill broke out of the makeshift prison camp in Pretoria and with the help of a local British resident - and some remarkable luck - smuggled himself by freight train over 300 miles to the neutral port of Lourenco Marques, in modern Mozambique. From there, he took ship to Durban and joined a local cavalry outfit, riding with Buller's army as it advanced on Pretoria. Probing ahead of the main column, together with the Duke of Marlborough (his cousin), he personally captured over 50 surrendering Boers. Back in Britain he now enjoyed hero status. His travails provided an ideal platform from which to contest the 1900 "Khaki" election.

---

[4] And indeed, they ultimately were: Young Winston, 1972.

Again he stood at Oldham and this time he won, albeit with a slim majority. Less than five years after Randolph Churchill's death, there was a Churchill in the House of Commons. Yet Winston took advantage of the autumn recess to pursue more commercial ambitions. He embarked upon an extended lecture tour across much of Britain and the United States that was solely about money. Until 1911, British Members of Parliament were not paid a salary, but the tour and its associated book sales earned him enough income, for awhile at least, to ignore such matters and instead turn to his central ambition: politics.

Churchill during his tour, 1900

In those early years, Winston Churchill cut an uneasy figure within the governing Conservative party. He was opposed to the Government's large scale military expenditure, and his classical economic leanings placed him firmly in the "free trade" camp as the Government moved towards a tariffs regime. He joined a maverick group of Conservative MP's called the "Hughligans" - after Hugh Cecil, their ringleader, often associating with Opposition Members and criticizing the Government from the wings.

He had made his first parliamentary speech in February of 1901, memorized from a carefully rehearsed draft. In future years he was to keep his notes with him, following an early and embarrassing mishap when his memory failed him. Churchill's powerful rhetorical oratory was thus always based on his writing. The set pieces were scripted beforehand.

When Balfour took over as Prime Minister from Campbell-Bannerman in 1903, trade protection became a prominent issue. Churchill's position on the subject, coupled with his reputation for sniping from the back-benches, dashed any hopes of a junior ministerial position. Indeed, Churchill was never to develop the tribal instincts that make for a loyal party man.

Frustrated and increasingly at odds with the Conservative leadership, Churchill crossed the floor of the House to join the Liberal benches on 31st May 1904.

It would be December 1905 before Balfour's weak Conservative government finally collapsed, ushering in a Liberal administration under Campbell-Bannerman. Churchill used this period to deliver waspish attacks on his former colleagues, mostly on the question of free trade. In doing so he created powerful enemies, some of whom would act to thwart him in years to come. Politically, he became close to David Lloyd-George, the radical Welsh Liberal, with whom he would form a powerful axis during the ensuing decade. His writing continued apace, notably with a well received biography of his father, published in 1906.

In the 1906 election he stood for the previously Conservative Manchester North West constituency and won the seat for the Liberals with a respectable majority. He was immediately given the position of Under Secretary of State for the Colonies, an office he was to hold for two years. It was Churchill's good fortune to represent his department in the House of Commons, because the more senior minister (Lord Elgin) sat in the Lords. He was therefore able to hone his political skills by presenting government policy in areas such as Transvaal home rule. Behind the scenes he would keep his civil servants busy, roaming across a whole swathe of issues, asking awkward questions, writing memoranda, putting forward a barrage of new ideas.

Politically, he was moving to the left. He strongly identified with the "New Liberalism" of the period, with its emphasis on active government and social justice. In 1908 he published an article entitled "The Untrodden Field in Politics", in which he argued for a minimum wage and public works to mitigate unemployment. This political transition is usually ascribed to his closeness with the older David Lloyd George, but this is a simplification. Churchill was maturing as a politician and a thinker, and such views represented an honest engagement with the issues and ideas of the day.

1908 proved to be a pivotal year for Churchill. His relationships with women had not been easy; he was often rather gauche in their company, and had twice been rejected in marriage. But when he met, for the second time, Clementine Hozier, they quickly fell in love and were married within the year. Their first child, Diana, was born in July of the following year. Clementine, herself from an aristocratic but impecunious background, would prove a loyal and loving wife. Importantly, with her powerful intellect and independent views (she would remain a Liberal throughout her life) she was a sounding board who would challenge and check her husband without hesitation. As the saying goes, "behind every great man...".

Winston and Clementine, 1908

1908 was also the year that saw Churchill's elevation to the cabinet at the remarkably early age of 32. Asquith, the new Liberal leader, admired Churchill's work and offered him the important post of President of the Board of Trade. His career nearly came badly unstuck however, because convention required those appointed to the cabinet to resign their parliamentary seats and seek a fresh mandate. Churchill lost his marginal Manchester constituency but was fortunate to be offered the Liberal candidacy in a safer by-election in Dundee, Scotland. Despite his "New Liberalism", he used the campaign to launch vitriolic attacks on the rival Labour Party. For all his radicalism, Churchill was never a socialist. It worked, and he won the seat with a decent majority.

In the cabinet he teamed up with Lloyd George to push through some of Britain's most progressive policies of the early 20th century, and together they were known as the "Radical Twins". The reforms included statutory minimum wages in key industries and an unemployment insurance scheme. He argued forcefully against the naval arms race with Germany, but lost his cabinet battle, with the result that the welfare reforms had instead to be paid for with tax rises. In turn, this prompted a constitutional clash with the House of Lords, which voted down the Liberal budget of 1909. It was not until the Parliament Act of August 1911, still in effect today, that this crisis was finally resolved. These debates would put Churchill firmly in the public eye. He relished the argument, delivering detailed and highly effective speeches at a series of public meetings around the country.

David Lloyd George

Conservative opinion of Churchill reached a new low, and even within his own party, his background meant that he was always regarded with some suspicion. Yet his stellar performance at the Board of Trade persuaded Asquith to appoint him Home Secretary, following the general election of January 1910. It was one of the great offices of state, and he was still just 34 years old.

Churchill's time at the Home Office marked the beginning of another transition in his thinking. Possibly because Asquith's government relied for support both from the Labour Party and from Irish nationalist MP's - whose views he deeply opposed, he began to associate again with figures in the Conservative Party. As Home Secretary as well, many of his decisions smacked of authoritarianism. Despite his views on social welfare he had little time for strikers and rioters - those who would disrupt the King's peace. On more than one occasion he authorized the use of troops against rioters. Yet in the case of the Tonypandy strikers, for which he was demonized by the Labour Party, this was precisely because he wished to ensure national control of the situation, rather than leave it to the amateurish local authorities. It is also worth noting his considerable efforts at penal and sentencing reform during the same period. As ever with Churchill, the man is more complex than he at first seems.

His move to the Admiralty (as First Lord – effectively making him minister for the Navy) in October of 1911 recognized his growing interest in military affairs. Asquith had taken him to a meeting of the Committee on Imperial Defense some weeks earlier and been impressed with Churchill's highly critical interventions. He probably felt that the Admiralty needed a shake up - war with Germany now seemed a distinct possibility. Yet viewed conventionally, this was a demotion. The likelihood is that Labour and Irish MP's were uneasy with Churchill's abrasive style at the Home Office; Asquith needed to keep them onside, while at the same time Churchill had a good command of military matters and was enthusiastic about the move. It seemed to make sense for all concerned.

Naturally, Churchill certainly upset the naval establishment. Working closely with the former First Sea Lord[5] (John "Jacky" Fisher, who was by now supposedly retired), he took on vested interests and modernized the fleet. This entailed arguing for more resources within the cabinet, thereby straining his relationship with Lloyd George. He pushed through the expansion of the Royal Naval Air Service and the development of submarines. By now Churchill was convinced that war was coming. The advocate of defense cuts in 1909 was now urging military expansion.

Though mostly focused on military affairs during this period, he also worked hard to find compromise on the difficult matter of Ireland. Unionist sentiment, strongly supported by the Conservative Party, was deeply hostile to the Irish Home Rule Bill. Churchill was not unsympathetic; at one stage he proposed regional devolution across the United Kingdom and throughout he was in secret talks with the Opposition. As events reached a boiling point in Belfast, with a threatened "Loyalist" revolt, the Government prepared for the worst. Churchill readied a naval squadron. Fortunately the crisis was (for the time being) averted; but once again, Churchill's name was mud in Conservative and Unionist circles.

Although the Third Home Rule Bill would become law in September 1914, the outbreak of war in Europe eclipsed the Irish crisis and its implementation was placed on hold during hostilities. With the British government still undecided about intervention against Germany, the Royal Navy was nonetheless fully deployed for battle. Churchill, and the navy he had nurtured, were ready for action.

New York State Senator Roosevelt

---

[5] "Sea Lords" were the most senior professional naval officers, the First Sea Lord being the Head of the Navy. "Lords" of the Admiralty were by contrast their political masters: effectively the naval ministerial team.

In 1910, FDR was elected to the New York State Senate, representing his home town of Hyde Park. The district had not elected a Democrat since 1884, but Roosevelt's family prestige and the Democratic favorability that year helped bring him to Albany.

Roosevelt's time in the State Senate often surprises those who know him only for his Presidency. Though his later Presidential run attracted the Catholic "white ethnic" vote, his time in the State Senate was actually focused on countering the influence of "white ethnic" leaders. For example, much of his efforts were devoted to breaking the influence of Irish Tammany Hall bosses and union leaders, who had held the Democratic Party in a stranglehold for over half a century. One of FDR's most successful moments came when he rallied the Democrats to defeat the Tammany candidate for one of New York's U.S. Senate seats.

FDR's reelection in 1912 further aligned him with this anti-Tammany, subtly anti-Irish faction of the Democratic Party. In that year, FDR was an early supporter of Woodrow Wilson for President, a man strongly opposed by Irish Catholics across the country. Wilson won the nomination, the Presidency, and later became the first Democratic President to be reelected since the Civil War.

President Woodrow Wilson

Chapter 7: The First World War

When World War I broke out against Europe, it seemed to directly refute the notion of the Bolsheviks that the proletariat would rise up as one internationally and engage in class warfare. Instead, members of socialist parties across Europe rallied around their flags to support their countries, even though Lenin and other Bolsheviks felt that the war would be just one more example of poorer classes fighting the bourgeoisie's "imperialist war", instead of uniting together to engage in class warfare. In the year before the war broke out, Lenin asserted, "The bourgeoisie incites the workers of one nation against those of another in the endeavour to keep them disunited. Class-conscious workers, realizing that the break-down of all the national barriers by capitalism is inevitable and progressive, are trying to help to enlighten and organize their fellow-workers from the backward countries."

Though Bolsheviks like Lenin opposed the war, at least in the manner it was being fought between belligerent nations, the war also provided an opportunity. While many were calling for the Russians to pull out of the war entirely, especially as Russian loses mounted, Lenin called instead for the people to "turn the imperialist war into a civil war." He wanted the people of Russia to use the opportunity of a distracted monarchy to rise up and overthrow the Romanovs.

Ironically, Lenin's push for continuing the war brought him into conflict with many of his fellow socialists, particularly Rosa Luxemburg. She was quick to point out that socialism or even democracy would not protect the Russian people from the Germans, but Lenin nevertheless maintained, "International unity of the workers is more important than the national." When the International Socialist Burean Conference rolled around in Brussels in 1915, Lenin dispatched Inessa Armand to fight those who supported peace, including Luxemburg, Plekhanov, Trotsky and Martov.

Churchill and the War

Storm clouds had been gathering in the years before the start of what would become The Great War. After Napoleon was finally defeated in 1815, the nations of Europe made their latest and greatest attempt to establish peace at Vienna. However, the Europeans continued to compete with each other across the world, and they established alliances to maintain some semblance of a balance of power. In 1873, German chancellor Otto van Bismarck reached an alliance with Austria-Hungary's despot and the Russian czar. The French signed alliances with Britain and Russia, who had left its previous alliance over tension brought about by Austria-Hungary's intervention in the Balkans. By then, Italy had joined the German alliance.

Although a couple of wars were fought on the European continent during the 19th century, an uneasy peace had mostly held across the continent after the Napoleonic Era. Nevertheless, countries across Europe had continued to conduct arms races against each other, an issue Churchill had come to find himself on both sides of. Britain had boasted the world's greatest navy for centuries, but Germany hoped to build its way to supremacy on the seas, and it would fall on Churchill to help ensure that didn't happen.

With men like Churchill anticipating a potential war, all that was missing was something to start the fire. The start of the chain of events occurred in 1908, when Austria-Hungary annexed

Bosnia-Herzegovina in the Balkan Peninsula, drawing it into dispute with Russia. The last straw came on 28 June 1914, when Archduke Franz Ferdinand, the heir to the throne of Austria-Hungary, was assassinated by a Serbian nationalist in Sarajevo, Bosnia. Austria-Hungary immediately issued ultimatums to Serbia that could not have possibly been met, and a month later they declared war on Serbia. In response to that, the Russians mobilized for war, and the Germans then mobilized in response to Russia days later. That brought in the French and British, both of whom declared war on Germany within a week. Thus, in the span of just a week, 6 European powers had declared war on each other, and half of them had no national interests in the Balkan Peninsula to begin with.

Nevertheless, with the outbreak of war, Churchill's style at the Admiralty became even more "hands on", to the extent of personally deploying units and composing signals to operational commanders. Such an approach was high risk: it generated resentment in the upper echelons of the service and meant that politically, he would be closely associated with any setbacks. His wife Clementine repeatedly warned him about this, but in reality this was part of his DNA.

Strategically, the most important activity by far was the Navy's blockade of Germany - a policy which by 1918 would constitute a major (some would argue the major) cause of her defeat. The blockade was imposed from day one of the war, and Churchill deserves credit for the Navy's readiness.

Tactically the picture was more mixed, with early embarrassment at the German bombardment of Scarborough in December 1914, a British victory off the Falklands in the same month, and a narrow defeat off the Dogger Bank in January 1915. Not content with sitting in the Admiralty, Churchill had travelled to Antwerp in October in order to personally supervise the defense of the city, deploying naval infantry to do so. Antwerp fell, and he was heavily criticized for it; yet a cooler examination of the battle reveals that British intervention bought vital time for retreats elsewhere.

It is hard to imagine Churchill having resisted the lure of the proposed Gallipoli[6] campaign. Despite the mythology this was not his idea, and although he was to champion it, other supporters included Asquith and Lord Kitchener, Secretary of State for War. The successful seizure of the straits and the arrival of an allied fleet at Constantinople may not have immediately knocked Turkey out of the war, but would certainly have represented a major strategic coup. Whether it could have been done is still subject to conjecture, but clearly, the two attempts to force the straits by naval power alone (February and March 1915) were a mistake. Again, whilst Churchill's proximity to operational decision making and his loudly proclaimed optimism would ensure opprobrium when plans went badly, the truth about his involvement is more subtle. In fact

---

[6] Also known as the Dardanelles campaign.

he had been skeptical about a naval-only attack, and it was Admiral Carden who had insisted that the plan would succeed.

In April, troops were landed against the by now thoroughly prepared Turkish defenses. Very quickly, the land campaign descended into the kind of attritional stalemate which had already frozen the Western Front in place. In London, Asquith faced a cabinet crisis and in May formed a wartime coalition with the Conservatives. Churchill was tainted - and loathed by many in the Conservative Party. He was demoted and given the sinecure position of Chancellor of the Duchy of Lancaster.

Crucially, he was placed on the Dardanelles Committee. It was this work, between May and November 1915, which perhaps warranted the most criticism. Churchill was slow to appreciate the hopelessness of the situation in Gallipoli, and when the casualties mounted, the campaign became unpopular, as did he. Ultimately disillusioned and feeling personally responsible, he resigned from the Government and sought an infantry command on the Western Front. Meanwhile at Westminster, Lloyd George took over as Prime Minister from Asquith in December; but even so, there was no prospect for Winston in a coalition involving the Conservatives.

As commander of a battalion in Belgium[7], Churchill spent some three months in the front line. Initially regarded with suspicion by many of his officers, he swiftly established a reputation for brave and imaginative leadership. He also went out of his way to ensure the welfare of his troops. He was frustrated however, and missed not having a greater say in the events of the day. The amalgamation of his battalion in May 1916 provided the excuse he needed to resign and return to Parliament. For the following year he busied himself as a backbencher, increasingly concerned about the conduct of the war, and in particular, the carnage on the Western Front. On 10 May 1917 he made a brilliant speech in Parliament, critiquing the allies' attritional strategy.

---

[7] 6th Battalion, Royal Scots Fusileers.

Churchill with the Royal Scots Fusiliers, 1916

Lloyd George understood that not only was Churchill an energetic and creative thinker, but he was also more dangerous on the back benches than in the Government. In the teeth of Conservative opposition, he appointed Churchill as Minister of Munitions - now a huge government department. Churchill brought fresh energy and imagination to Britain's wartime production during this critical period. He reorganized the department, intervened to ensure that factory workers' grievances were properly addressed, and made it his business to visit the army regularly in France. In doing so he secured the respect of Field Marshal Haig and they worked effectively together. They ensured, for example, that tank production and delivery was given high priority - an important factor in the final allied offensive of August 1918.

Churchill's domestic life remained mostly settled during the war years. Clementine had proved his sternest critic but also his most loyal friend. His third child Sarah was born whilst he was in Antwerp (son Randolph had arrived in 1911) and Marigold was born at the end of 1918. He had become very down over the Gallipoli disaster and discovered painting as a means of alleviating these "Black Dog" moods. It was a pastime he was to enjoy for the rest of his life.

World War I is best remembered for its trench war stalemate, but by the summer of 1918, the Allied powers were successful in a counteroffensive that pushed the Germans backward on the

Western Front. That September, Bulgaria signed an armistice with the Allied powers that ceded control of the Balkans and cut off German supplies. Shortly after, the Ottoman Empire surrendered, while some of the lands in Austria-Hungary's empire openly revolted and declared their independence. Germany's Kaiser was forced into exile at the beginning of that winter, and the Germans famously signed an armistice at 11:00 a.m. on 11 November 1918. The First World War had finally ended.

The Armistice found Churchill a successful minister, a controversial figure chastened by war but hungry for power and renown.

Assistant Secretary of the Navy Roosevelt

FDR's political rise hadn't gone unnoticed either. Wilson appreciated Roosevelt's early support, and in 1913 Roosevelt left the State Senate to serve as Wilson's Assistant Secretary of the Navy. At the time, the position seemed a relatively minor one, but the breakout of World War I increased its importance, and one of Roosevelt's most important accomplishments as Assistant Secretary was the creation of the Navy Reserve.

Assistant Secretary of the Navy Roosevelt

Nevertheless, after just a year serving as Assistant Secretary, Roosevelt hoped to take on Tammany Hall again, running against the Tammany-backed candidate for a U.S. Senate seat in New York. Wilson opposed this decision, having realized that Irish Catholics and union members would be crucial to his reelection in 1916. Wilson understood that his election in 1912 was largely due to Theodore Roosevelt's Bull Moose third party run, which had divided the Republican vote. The President did not want one of his cabinet secretaries giving New Yorkers the impression that he, too, wanted to topple Tammany influence.

Roosevelt lost the Senate nomination in 1914. Wilson was pleased, and Roosevelt learned a lesson. From then on, he toned down his opposition to Tammany Hall. Thankfully for FDR, his relationship with Wilson was not significantly strained by his failed Senate run. Roosevelt remained the Assistant Secretary of the Navy until almost the end of Wilson's second term. By 1917, FDR could see the writing on the wall with Germany's unrestricted submarine warfare in the Atlantic, and he wanted to prepare the U.S. Navy for battle. However, Wilson was still not ready for a potential American commitment to war, shooting down FDR's suggestion. Once America entered the war, it had to scramble to mobilize. It was a lesson that served FDR well 20 years later.

The February Revolution, 1917

The Bolsheviks' hopes for a Russian Civil War received a catalyst from a strange place. In September of 1915, Tsar Nicholas II dismissed his generals on the Eastern Front and took over military command himself. Thus, as the number of battles lost grew, his reputation and popularity among the people fell. By 1917, it was clear that the Russian Army would never be able to sustain further involvement in the war, having already lost almost 8 million soldiers to death, injury and capture. With that, the Russian people began to cry out against the privations of the war. Factory workers staged strikes for higher wages to pay the ever inflating cost of food for their families. At the same time, people in Petrograd rioted in the streets, vandalizing shops and demanding food that the government simply did not have.

Had he been wiser, Nicholas might have appealed to the people, or met with the Duma to work out some sort of solution to the shortages. However, he had been raised with the understanding that the main work of a Tsar was to preserve the monarchy for his son. Thus, he decided on the very inopportune moment of late February, 1917 to try to disband the Duma and regain absolute power. When the Duma refused to disband, the High Commander of the army appealed to Nicholas, suggesting that he should abdicate before a full scale revolution broke out. Some suggested that the Tsar's cousin, Grand Duke Michael Alexandrovich would make an excellent replacement. He refused, however, and on March 1, Nicholas was forced to leave and was replaced with a Provisional Government which originally consisted of a mishmash of parliamentary figures and members of revolutionary councils that had been elected by workers, soldiers and peasants.

In almost no time at all, Russia's old monarchy had been dissolved.

Creating a Provisional Government

When Alexander Kerensky, the prime minster put in place by the Mensheviks (social democrats and opponents of Lenin's Bolsheviks), freed all the political prisoners in Russia, Stalin returned to St. Petersburg to a hero's welcome. He was immediately given back his job as editor of Pravda, now the national paper of Russia. Together with the Mensheviks, he published articles designed to prepare the people of the country for a future socialist revolution while still supporting the provisional government.

With the Tsar now out of power, Russia's socialist parties moved to fill the vacuum, as leaders like Stalin and Lenin returned to Russia from exile. While on a train from Switzerland to Russia, Lenin completed work on what became known as his famous April Theses, and he read them aloud as soon as he entered Petrograd on April 3rd. In it he outlined his plans for the immediate future:

1. In view of the undoubted honesty of the mass of rank and file representatives of revolutionary defencism who accept the war only as a necessity and not as a means of conquest, in view of their being deceived by the bourgeoisie, it is necessary most thoroughly, persistently, patiently to explain to them their error, to explain the inseparable connection between capital and the imperialist war, to prove that without the overthrow of capital it is impossible to conclude the war with a really democratic, non-oppressive peace.

2. The peculiarity of the present situation in Russia is that it represents a transition from the first stage of the revolution - which, because of the inadequate organization and insufficient class-consciousness of the proletariat, led to the assumption of power by the bourgeoisie - to its second stage which is to place power in the hands of the proletariat and the poorest strata of the peasantry.

3. No support to the Provisional Government; exposure of the utter falsity of all its promises, particularly those relating to the renunciation of annexations. Unmasking, instead of admitting, the illusion-breeding "demand" that this government, a government of capitalist, should cease to be imperialistic.

4. Recognition of the fact that in most of the Soviets of Workers' Deputies our party constitutes a minority, and a small one at that, in the face of the bloc of all the petty bourgeois opportunist elements who have yielded to the influence of the bourgeoisie.

It must be explained to the masses that the Soviet of Workers' Deputies is the only possible form of revolutionary government and that, therefore, our task is, while this government is submitting to the influence of the bourgeoisie, to present a patient, systematic, and persistent analysis of its errors and tactics, an analysis especially adapted to the practical needs of the masses.

5. Not a parliamentary republic - a return to it from the Soviet of Workers' Deputies would be a step backward - but a republic of Soviets of Workers', Agricultural Labourers' and Peasants' Deputies throughout the land, from top to bottom.

Abolition of the police, the army, the bureaucracy. All officers to be elected and to be subject to recall at any time, their salaries not to exceed the average wage of a competent worker.

6. In the agrarian program, the emphasis must be shifted to the Soviets of Agricultural Laborers' Deputies [including]

   a. Confiscation of private lands.

   b. Nationalization of all lands in the country, and management of such lands by local Soviets of Agricultural Labourers' and Peasants' Deputies.

   c. A separate organization of Soviets of Deputies of the poorest peasants.

   d. Creation of model agricultural establishments out of large estates.

7. Immediate merger of all the banks in the country into one general national bank, over which the Soviet of Workers' Deputies should have control.

8. Not the "introduction" of Socialism as an immediate task, but the immediate placing of the Soviet of Workers' Deputies in control of social production and distribution of goods.

9. Party tasks [include] Immediate calling of a party convention and Changing the party program, mainly:

   a. Concerning imperialism and the imperialist war.

   b. Concerning our attitude toward the state, and our demand for a 'commune state."

   c. Amending our antiquated minimum program.

10. Rebuilding the International. Taking the initiative in the creation of a revolutionary International, an International against the social-chauvinists and against the "center".

Although the turmoil had been limited to Russia so far, and the Theses were written about how to immediately create a socialist state in Russia, it's clear that Lenin envisioned an international revolution even at this early date. As one historian characterized his thinking in 1917, "Lenin made his revolution for the sake of Europe, not for the sake of Russia, and he expected Russia's preliminary revolution to be eclipsed when the international revolution took place. Lenin did not invent the iron curtain."

Lenin's April Theses were among the most radical writings of his life to date, and both Mensheviks and fellow Bolsheviks were taken aback. The Theses were roundly condemned by the Mensheviks (one of whom described them as the "ravings of a madman"), and initially the Theses were supported by only one prominent Bolshevik, Alexandra Kollontai.

Kollontai

One of the people that were concerned about Lenin's insistence on an immediate revolution was Stalin. Stalin's and his fellow Mensheviks' belief that the Russian people needed time to adjust before becoming completely committed to socialism brought him into conflict with his mentor, Lenin, who was fomenting massive uprisings by the workers against the ruling class around them. Whereas Stalin saw socialism as a plan in progress, Lenin wanted immediate action against both the landed aristocracy and the owners of large factories. While he had always been fascinated by Lenin's ideals, Stalin was usually too pragmatic to begin a venture without an assurance of success.

Though Stalin and other Bolsheviks still believed that the revolution should be a bourgeoise revolution, the Theses at least presented a party platform and a banner under which revolutionaries could rally and united. Thus, after wrestling with the issue for ten days, Stalin wrote a scathing article in which he dismissed the work of Kerensky, Victor Chernov and the Provisional Government as a betrayal of all the revolution was about, instead supporting Lenin and urging the peasants to rise up immediately. He further instructed them to begin by forming local committees that would confiscate large, privately owned estates and turn them over to the peasants that worked on them.

The chaos continued when Alexander Kerensky, the new head of the Provisional Government, launched yet another military offensive against the Germans in July of 1917. Soldiers deserted by the thousands, with many of them carrying their government issued weapons back to the estates where they lived. They often used these guns to threaten or even kill their landlords so that they could have their land. They also burned stately mansions and moved ancient boundary stones to create new, smaller farms for the peasants themselves to own.

Kerensky

Alarmed by the rioting and believing that it was a result of the impact Lenin and other revolutionaries were having on the common people, Kerensky outlawed the Bolsheviks and tried to round up its members, outlandishly accusing them of being German agents. Trotsky famously defended Lenin and other Bolsheviks against the charge, exhorting, "An intolerable atmosphere has been created, in which you, as well as we, are choking. They are throwing dirty accusations at Lenin and Zinoviev. Lenin has fought thirty years for the revolution. I have fought [for] twenty years against the oppression of the people. And we cannot but cherish a hatred for German militarism . . . I have been sentenced by a German court to eight months' imprisonment for my struggle against German militarism. This everybody knows. Let nobody in this hall say that we are hirelings of Germany." Luckily for Lenin, he got wind of the threat well enough ahead of time to escape to Finland, where he completed work on *State and Revolution*, an outline of the government he hoped to one day see in Russia.

Trotsky

October Revolution

As the rioting was going on back at home, Kerensky's July Offensive failed miserably, and he came into conflict with his new general, Lavr Kornilov, over policies related to discipline and production. When Kornilov sent the troops under his command to march on Kerensky's headquarters in Petrograd, Kerensky had to appeal to the Bolsheviks for Red Guards to protect his capitol city. Lenin reluctantly agreed and immediately recruited more than 25,000 soldiers to protect the government he so vehemently opposed. When Kornilov's troops saw the rows of dug in Red Guards, they refused to advance, and Kornilov surrendered to the palace police.

Realizing that he now had the Provisional Government largely at his mercy, Lenin returned to Russia in October and set up a party headquarters in Smolny Institute for Girls in St. Petersburg. From there, he quietly ordered that the Provisional Government be deposed and the Winter Palace vacated. On the evening of October 25, the Second All-Russian Congress of Soviets met at the Smolny Institute to establish a new government. While there were initially some disagreements over the overthrow of the Provisional Government, Martov's Mensheviks and Lenin's Bolsheviks eventually agreed to share power. Ironically, after all the drama that had surrounded the earlier months of that year, the October Revolution went largely unnoticed. As Lenin had written a month earlier, "The peaceful development of any revolution is, generally speaking, extremely rare and difficult ... but ... a peaceful development of the revolution is possible and probable if all power is transferred to the Soviets. The struggle of parties for power within the Soviets may proceed peacefully, if the Soviets are made fully democratic." It seemed that way in October.

Lenin arrived at the meeting the next evening to thunderous applause, appearing without a disguise for the first time since July. Famous American journalist John Reed, who would later chronicle the Russian Revolution in his critically acclaimed book, *Ten Days That Shook The World*, described Lenin for readers. "A short, stocky figure, with a big head set down in his shoulders, bald and bulging. Little eyes, a snubbish nose, wide, generous mouth, and heavy chin; clean-shaven now, but already beginning to bristle with the well-known beard of his past and future. Dressed in shabby clothes, his trousers much too long for him. Unimpressive, to be the idol of a mob, loved and revered as perhaps few leaders in history have been. A strange popular leader—a leader purely by virtue of intellect; colourless, humourless, uncompromising and detached, without picturesque idiosyncrasies—but with the power of explaining profound ideas in simple terms, of analysing a concrete situation. And combined with shrewdness, the greatest intellectual audacity."

Beginning his speech with "We shall now proceed to construct the Socialist order!", at the meeting, Lenin proposed a "Decree on Peace" calling for an end of the war, and a "Decree on Land" announcing that all property owned by large land owners and the aristocracy would be given to the peasants. Both decrees passed with little dissension. Next, the new government elected a Bolshevik majority to the Council of People's Commissars, with the Mensheviks joining the government a few weeks later. Lenin was soon elected Chairman of the Council, making him head of the government, though he had originally intended for the position to go to Trotsky, who declined because he worried his Jewish ethnicity would pose problems.

In recognition of his contribution, the now totally empowered Lenin appointed Stalin the Commissar of Nationalities, joking with him about his meteoric rise to power. As Commissar, Stalin was in charge of all the non-Russian people in the country, including Buriats, Byelorussians, Georgians, Tadzhiks, Ukrainians and Yakuts, nearly half the country's population. The spoiled little boy who'd been forced to speak Russian and had been teased about his appearance was now a bitter, angry man with nearly unlimited power. The combination would not make for a pretty outcome.

Initially, however, it looked like all would be well for these foreigners under Russian control. He concluded his famous Helsinki address of 1917 with these words of encouragement and promises of support:

"Comrades! Information has reached us that your country is experiencing approximately the same crisis of power as Russia experienced on the eve of the October Revolution. Information has reached us that attempts are being made to frighten you too with the bogey of famine, sabotage, and so on. Permit me to tell you on the basis of the practical experience of the revolutionary movement in Russia that these dangers, even if real, are by no means insuperable! These dangers can be overcome if you act resolutely and without faltering. In the midst of war and economic disruption, in the midst of the revolutionary movement which is flaring up in the West and of the increasing victories of the workers' revolution in Russia, there are no dangers or difficulties that could withstand your onslaught. In such a situation only one power, socialist power, can maintain itself and conquer. In such a situation only one kind of tactics can be effective, the tactics of Danton—audacity, audacity and again audacity! And if you should need our help, you will have it—we shall extend you a fraternal hand. Of this you may rest assured."

Unfortunately, the non-Russian peoples who heard or read this speech remained unconvinced. They were not so much interested in Russian help as they were national determination. Therefore they proved to be a constant source of stress to the new Commissar, setting up their own governments, opposing Bolshevik policy, and overall acting with the self-determination they had been promised, as long as they determined to join the new Union of Soviet Socialist Republics.

Faced with this level of opposition to his and the other Bolsheviks' plans, Stalin took a different tact. Accusing the new independent governments of being under the control of "the bourgeoisie," he agreed with Lenin that a more centralized government was needed. As the Russian Civil War played out during the early 1920s, Stalin became more involved in military matters while Lenin continued to focus on politics.

Chapter 8: Politics and Polio

Vice Presidential Candidate

After World War I, Wilson faced stiff resistance to his post-war policies back at home, and he suffered a stroke in the middle of his second term while trying to rally support for initiatives like the League of Nations. With Wilson debilitated, Roosevelt resigned from the Navy in 1920 to run for Vice President on the Democratic ticket under Governor James Cox of Ohio. At 38 years old, Roosevelt was one of the youngest people to ever run for Vice President, but he brought plenty of political experience, as well as foreign policy accolades (like his support for the League of Nations) to the Democratic ticket, something Cox only mildly supported. Like his previous political career, these positions again put Roosevelt in confrontation with Irish Catholics, who opposed the League of Nations because it did not admit the then-rebelling Republic of Ireland. The country was recognized as part of Great Britain.

Cox and Roosevelt lost the election of 1920 to Warren G. Harding. It was probably a blessing in disguise for Roosevelt for several reasons. As it would turn out, he'd have to battle illness during the decade, and the Republican policies under Harding, Coolidge and Hoover contributed to the events that led to Roosevelt's eventual election as President.

FDR Contracts Polio

After losing the Vice Presidency, Roosevelt's political career was hardly shattered. The loss was not blamed on FDR, and he gained popularity within the Democratic Party. Another event, however, put Roosevelt's future in doubt. In 1921, while at his family's summer home in Campobello Island in Canada, Roosevelt contracted an illness that was diagnosed as polio. While there is still some question as to exactly what the illness was, Roosevelt was paralyzed from the waist down.

Roosevelt was understandably devastated, especially because polio was an illness usually contracted during childhood. He initially refused to accept the diagnosis and spent the next few years searching for a cure. Most famously, he tried recuperating at a spa in Warm Springs, Georgia, but to no avail. Roosevelt would be bound to a wheelchair for the rest of his life. He used leg braces and crutches to move, but he could never walk independently again.

Chapter 9: Return of Conservative Churchill, 1918-24

Lloyd-George's coalition won the December 1918 election with ease, and Churchill was returned in Dundee, having campaigned on radical issues such as the 40 hour work week and the nationalization of the railways. In doing so he had studiously avoided the anti-German jingoism which had characterized much of the election.

Churchill was now given the twin ministries of Air and War, immediately acting to defuse a tense dispute which had arisen over army demobilization. He was the principle politician behind the "Ten Year Rule" - an assumption about world peace which was designed to facilitate substantial defense cuts. As had been the case in 1909, Churchill the warmonger was nothing of the sort when he perceived that the threat to Britain was waning.

One aspect of Churchill's search for defense savings was his advocacy of tactical airpower as a means of controlling large areas, such as Mesopotamia (modern day Iraq). Modern critics often criticize Churchill for Britain's plans to use gas and attacks on civilians. Without superimposing 21st century ethics on early 20th century history, it is a matter of record that Churchill was furious about the reported attacks on civilians, and that his proposal was only for the use of non-lethal tear gas on rebellious tribesmen[8].

He was bullish however, on the question of Russia. Deeply hostile to Bolshevism, Churchill argued for continued military intervention and considered resigning when the Anglo-Russian treaty was signed in November 1920.

The security situation in Ireland was also causing concern during this period. The deployment of the notorious "Black and Tans" in the summer of 1920, and the Government's initial tolerance of their atrocities can largely be attributed to Churchill. A settlement was reached with the establishment of the Free State under the terms of the 1921 Anglo Irish Treaty. By then Secretary of State for the Colonies, Churchill was instrumental in the negotiations. In doing so he established a strong rapport with Michael Collins, who went out of his way to thank Churchill for his contribution. But the shameful tactics employed during 1920-21 would not be readily forgotten in Ireland.

Churchill's move to the Colonial Office in February 1921 brought him into the tangled web of Middle Eastern affairs. In a series of skillfully managed diplomatic initiatives, he was able to hammer out the basis for a state structure, much of which survives to this day. Hence the establishment of Trans-Jordan and Iraq. Although sympathetic to Zionist ambitions, he did not go further than the Balfour Declaration of 1917, which recognized that a Jewish homeland should be created within the British Mandate of Palestine. As with Ireland however, the underlying tensions and disagreements of the region would not be resolved by Churchill's attempts at compromise and quasi-imperialism. In a sense, it was a thankless task, and he knew it: ever the pragmatist, in 1918 he had advocated a U.S. mandate in Palestine, rather than a British one!

---

[8] In fact even this proposal was ultimately rejected.

At the same time he was coping with personal tragedy at home. In April 1921, Clementine's brother committed suicide, and in May his mother died suddenly. Catastrophically, his infant daughter Marigold succumbed to septicemia in August. Thankfully for his personal life, 1922 would bring the joy of a new daughter, (Mary, born in September) and a splendid new home at Chartwell in Kent. Although Clementine did not immediately take to Chartwell, this was the first family home they had lived in since their marriage. Winston himself loved it, developing an interest in gardening and spending much of his income on improvements.

However, the year would also bring political defeat. In October, Lloyd George went to the country and the divided Liberal party was badly beaten. Churchill, ill with appendicitis for most of the campaign, lost his Dundee seat. To lick his wounds, he travelled to France, painting and preparing his multi-volume history of the First World War. He would not re-enter the fray for another year.

In December 1923, Baldwin, the new Conservative Party leader, called an election. Churchill stood in Leicester as a "Liberal Free Trader". Hostile to the Labour Party and disillusioned with the hopelessly split Liberal Party, Churchill was moving rightwards towards the Conservatives. Yet he would not endorse Baldwin's position on tariffs. He lost by a big margin.

The following March he fought a by-election in central London, this time as an "Independent anti-Socialist". Again he lost, but by only a whisker; and in the 1924 general election the local Conservatives invited him to fight the seat of Epping as a "Constitutionalist". Baldwin had changed his position on trade tariffs, and Churchill was back in the party in all but name.

Baldwin, anxious to prevent the mercurial and influential Churchill from slipping back into Lloyd-George's orbit, offered him the role of Chancellor of the Exchequer. A shocked Churchill accepted the post, confessing to Baldwin that he still possessed his father's Chancellor's robe. The politician with nine lives was back again.

Chapter 10: Stalin Takes Power, 1917-1924

Lenin and Stalin in the early 1920s

Lenin Secures the Revolution

Having seen how easily a multi-generational dynasty fell, Lenin was obviously concerned about keeping the new Soviet regime safe. To this end, he established "The Whole-Russian Extraordinary Commission for Combating Counter-Revolution and Sabotage" in the last weeks of 1917. Known colloquially as the Cheka (Extraordinary Commission), it soon became as feared by non-socialists as the Tsar's secret police had ever been. In addition to monitoring the movements of anyone opposing the government, the Cheka also enforced censorship laws against non-socialist newspapers.

While Lenin wanted Russia out of the war, he initially hoped to retain the land it had lost to the Germans. He worked with Trotsky, who had taken the post of Commissar for Foreign Affairs, to formulate a Russo-German treaty in which each country would agree to return any land gained from the other during the war. When this failed, he had to concede much of the Russian countryside to the Germans in return for pulling the Russians out of the war. The Treaty of Brest-Litovsk officially removed Russia from the conflict on March 3, 1918. However, it also resulted in Germany being so close to Petrograd that the government had to move its capital to Moscow.

Lenin and Fritz Platten

In spite of the Cheka's best efforts, those who opposed Lenin and the Bolsheviks were still out there, and they were gunning for Lenin, literally. In January 1918, gunmen shot at Lenin and Fritz Platten as they sat in an automobile after Lenin had given a speech, which Lenin survived after Platten pushed him down and shielded him. But the most famous assassination attempt would come in August 1918, when a supporter of the Socialist Revolutionary Party, Fanya Kaplan, approached Lenin as he sat in an automobile. After calling to him to get his attention, she fired at him three times, hitting him once in the arm and once in the jaw and neck. Though the wounds rendered him unconscious, Lenin survived the shooting, and fearful of people at the hospital who might try to finish the job, he returned to the Kremilin and ordered physicians to come there to treat him where he felt safe. Ultimately, doctors refused to perform surgery given the precarious position of the bullet in his neck. Pravda used the attempt for propaganda purposes, reporting, "Lenin, shot through twice, with pierced lungs spilling blood, refuses help and goes on his own. The next morning, still threatened with death, he reads papers, listens, learns, and observes to see that the engine of the locomotive that carries us towards global revolution has not stopped working..."

Fanya Kaplan

Despite that, Soviet officials began to downplay the attack, and many across Russia never learned of it. Though he survived the attack, the bullets were left in place and continued to erode his health. However, Lenin kept working and appearing in public, determined to keep the public ignorant of how weak his condition was becoming. This was important because Lenin was increasingly viewed as the embodiment of the new regime, and it was feared that his death could cause everything to crumble. One former Tsarist wrote as much, reporting after the attempt, "As it happens, the attempt to kill Lenin has made him much more popular than he was. One hears a great many people, who are far from having any sympathy with the Bolsheviks, saying that it would be an absolute disaster if Lenin had succumbed to his wounds, as it was first thought he would. And they are quite right, for, in the midst of all this chaos and confusion, he is the backbone of the new body politic, the main support on which everything rests."

The Bolsheviks may have downplayed the assassination attempt publicly, but they were privately plotting retaliation on a massive scale. Two weeks before Kaplan's attempt on Lenin's life, the Petrograd Cheka chief Moisei Uritsky had been assassinated, and now Stalin suggested to Lenin that they should engage in "open and systematic mass terror…[against] those responsible." Thus, the Cheka, under the instruction of Stalin, launched what later came to be known as the "Red Terror" in response to the assassination attempt. In the weeks that followed, more than 800 people were executed, including the entire Romanov family. This however, was just the beginning. As the Bolsheviks, known popularly as the Red Russians fought an ongoing war against those who opposed socialism (the White Russians), more than 18,000 people were executed on charges related to opposing Lenin and his rule. While historians have often debated the extent of Lenin's personal involvement in the executions, Trotsky himself later asserted that it was Lenin who authorized the execution of the Russian Royal Family.

Victims of the Red Terror

Unfortunately, bullets weren't all that was killing the Russian common people. While the Whites and Reds engaged in a civil war that would last for nearly 7 years, ordinary Russians were starving due to war time communism measures that allowed the Soviet government to confiscate food for soldiers from peasant farms with little or no payment. When the farmers retaliated by growing fewer crops, the Cheka responded by executing or imprisoning the offending peasants. However, even the Cheka could not cause plants to grow, and during the Famine of 1921, more than 5 million Russians starved to death in and near their own homes. This tragedy, along with the civil unrest it provoked, led Lenin to institute the New Economic Policy to rejuvenate the both agriculture and industry.

In formulating his economic policies, Lenin asserted, "We must show the peasants that the organisation of industry on the basis of modern, advanced technology, on electrification, which will provide a link between town and country, will put an end to the division between town and country, will make it possible to raise the level of culture in the countryside and to overcome, even in the most remote corners of land, backwardness, ignorance, poverty, disease, and barbarism." Of course, to Lenin that meant total State control over industry, and he implemented a system in which every industry was overseen by one ruling official granted all the deciding power over any disputes, thereby completely curbing workers' self-management rights.

A propagandist picture that reads, "Comrade Lenin Cleanses the Earth of Filth"

Lenin's first non-political interest was in bringing electricity to all of Russia, so that the homes and factories could be modernized. Disappointed with the lack of progress made by factories under their own power, Lenin made the first of many moves to expand government control over private lives by placing businesses under the supervision of Soviet committees. These committees would evaluate everything from worker rights to productivity to the flow of materials. They would then report to the government, who would, it was hoped, take steps to help the factories improve their productivity.

Having established a plan for economic improvements, Lenin turned his attention to social issues. First, he instituted a system of free health care for all Russians, as well as a widespread system of public education. With the encouragement of both his wife and his mistress, he encouraged the government to grant women the right to vote, and to encourage them to take advantage of higher education to train to enter the work force.

Stalin Fights the Russian Civil War

Stalin's military strategy was as effective as it was ruthless. Prior to his successful battle against the White Army at Tsaritsyn, he met with the local leaders on a boat tied up along the shore of the Volga River. It is rumored that he interviewed them thoroughly and then sent the ones he believed to be loyal back to their homes and offices. The ones whose loyalty he questioned were summarily shot and thrown in the river.

Stalin's desire for blood was fed by the assassination of Moisei Uritsky and the attempt on the life of Lenin himself in August, 1918. In a telegram to the badly wounded Lenin on August 31, Stalin committed himself to revenge:

> "Having learned of the villainous attempt of the hirelings of the bourgeoisie on the life of Comrade Lenin, the world's greatest revolutionary and the tried and tested leader and teacher of the proletariat, the Military Council of the North Caucasian Military Area is answering this vile attempt at assassination by instituting open and systematic mass terror against the bourgeoisie and its agents."

Lenin passed Stalin's recommendation on to Felix Dzerzhinsky, the head of Soviet state security, who in turn instituted the famous Red Terror the next day. The Bolsheviks began by rounding up 500 former aristocrats and their families and summarily executing them. This practicing of rooting out and executing perceived enemies of the state continued over the next two months until, by the end of October that year, more than 12,000 people had been killed and another 6,000 put into state prisons.

The unintended consequence of this genocide was that the Bolsheviks government became increasingly unpopular with the common Russian people. While they supported the ideas of freedom and brotherhood in general, they were not terribly sanguine about seeing more and more people around them hauled from their homes and shot. Many could sense the mania in the air and they wanted no part of it.

Following the Kronstadt Uprising in which Soviet military men and civilians teamed up to call for an end to the random slaughter of their countrymen, Lenin loosened up the government's control on economic policy. He even instituted the New Economic Policy, which allowed farmers to once again sell their produce in local markets. Those who needed to could even employ others to work for them without falling under the suspicion of being wealthy landowners. Those who did not farm were also allowed more freedom to own and run private businesses, including small factories.

While Stalin agreed with the New Economic Policy, others did not, and fighting to keep it alive began to take its toll of Lenin's health. Thus, in April of 1922, he met with other party leaders and asked that Stalin be appointed the first General Secretary of the Soviet Union. No one thought much of this move since Lenin appeared to still be in complete charge of the party, and it passed with little discussion. However, when Lenin suffered a stroke a few months later and was left paralyzed, Stalin was poised to take the reins.

The Death of Lenin

One of Stalin's powers as General Secretary allowed him to dismiss any party members he deemed useless or disloyal. Coincidentally, he quickly discovered the most of the followers of his arch rival, Leon Trotsky, fell into this category. Therefore, he was able to remove from party participation thousands of otherwise loyal members. He replaced them with members whom he knew to be loyal to him, and whose continued loyalty he could count on, since their comfortable positions depended on it.

In April of 1922, doctors finally decided to remove the bullet in Lenin's neck, but after a month spent resting and recovering, Lenin returned to his grueling schedule. This proved to be too much for his fragile physical state and he suffered a stroke just a month later. Though it affected his speech and his movement on the right side, he began to gradually recover by June and made the imprudent choice of going back to work. In addition to resuming duties in August, he also delivered a series of long speeches in November.

After the first stroke, weakened by his physical condition, Lenin fell prey to Stalin's ambition. In October of 1922, the Central Committee voted to accept Stalin's foreign trade policy instead of the one put forward by Lenin. Seeing the handwriting on the wall, Lenin contacted Trotsky and suggested that they team up to try to hold Stalin in check. Trotsky agreed and together they saw Stalin's policy overturned at the next committee meeting.

Unfortunately for Lenin, he had employed Stalin's wife, Nadya, as his secretary. She found a copy of the letter he sent to Trotsky and shared its contents with her husband. He in turn called Lenin's wife, Nadezhda, and berated her over the phone for allowing her weak and obviously delusional husband to write such a letter. This phone call sealed Stalin's fate in Lenin's eyes, and he dictated a letter in which he suggested that Stalin was not fit to take his place as the party's leader.

Sensing death was coming after the first stroke, Lenin began dictating instructions on how he would like the Soviet government to be continued, comprising what came to be known as Lenin's Testament near the end of 1922. In addition to dictating how the Soviet government should be structured, it was particularly notable in its criticism of several high-ranking officials, including Stalin, Trotsky, Grigory Zinoviev, Lev Kamenev, and Nikolai Bukharin. Lenin was extremely concerned about Stalin, who had become Communist Party's General Secretary in 1922. In it he compared Stalin negatively to Trotsky, saying,

> "Comrade Stalin, having become General Secretary, has concentrated an enormous

power in his hands; and I am not sure that he always knows how to use that power with sufficient caution. On the other hand, Comrade Trotsky, as was proved by his struggle against the Central Committee in connection with the question of the People's Commissariat of Ways and Communications, is distinguished not only by his exceptional abilities – personally he is, to be sure, the most able man in the present Central Committee – but also by his too far-reaching self-confidence and a disposition to be too much attracted by the purely administrative side of affairs."

Lenin completed this letter on Christmas Day, 1922. However, a few days later, perhaps concerned that he had not made his concerns sufficiently clear, he added the following postscript.

"Stalin is too rude, and this fault, entirely supportable in relations among us Communists, becomes insupportable in the office of General Secretary. Therefore, I propose to the comrades to find a way to remove Stalin from that position and appoint to it another man who in all respects differs from Stalin only in superiority – namely, more patient, more loyal, more polite and more attentive to comrades, less capricious, etc. This circumstance may seem an insignificant trifle, but I think that from the point of view of preventing a split and from the point of view of the relation between Stalin and Trotsky which I discussed above, it is not a trifle, or it is such a trifle as may acquire a decisive significance."

Lenin simply burned his body out by continuing to push it to its physical limits, and he suffered a second stroke in December of that same year, which partly paralyzed the right side of his body. The third and final stroke in March of 1923 proved his final undoing, rendering him mute and bedridden.

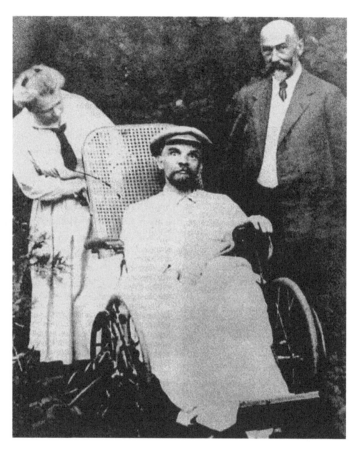

Lenin after his third stroke

On January 21, 1924, Lenin's body finally gave out, and he died that night in his estate at Gorki at just 53 years old. For four days his body lay in state, during which time nearly a million mourners passed through to see it. By then, Petrograd had been renamed Leningrad. Most famously, Lenin's body was embalmed and placed for public display in Lenin's Mausoleum, where plenty of visitors can still pass by his body and view it each day. It is estimated that over 100 million have viewed his body in the last 88 years.

Site of Lenin's death

Consolidating Power

Lenin was the unquestioned head of the new Soviet Union, and upon his death he had firmly expressed the desire to make sure Stalin didn't concentrate power and control over the young Communist nation. Of course, that's precisely what ended up happening. So how and why did Lenin's Testament go unheeded?

When Lenin's widow unearthed the document for Soviet officials, it was quickly disregarded and suppressed by Stalin, Kamenev, and Zinoviev, the ruling troika that Lenin had disparaged. Other leaders went about making sure the Testament had no effect, with Trotsky publishing an article countering its importance and asserting that they were not a will and had not technically been violated. It was a stance Trotsky himself would come to regret in ensuing years as his opposition to Stalin increased.

While the letter made clear Lenin's intentions, it did not have the force of law behind it, especially with the remaining Soviet leaders asserting that it was not a final will. Since Lenin died before he could use his own personal leadership to enforce his wishes, Stalin became the preeminent Soviet leader. At the same time, his battle with Lenin had given him a sense of the bigger picture, and he now saw the wisdom of moving more slowly, especially when dealing with the common people. Therefore, he initially left the New Economic Policy in place and even allowed the farmers to buy up land around them to expand their farms. These larger landowners were known at kulaks, meaning "fists" for the tight way in which they held on to their land.

On the political front, Stalin had other things on his mind. As the General Secretary of the Soviet Union, he courted the favor of Lev Kamenev and Grigory Zinoviev, two powerful members of the Politburo, to keep Trotsky in check. He encouraged rumors that Trotsky would probably oust them if he came to power so that he could put his own people in power. He also encouraged a sense of his superiority, along with theirs, against the upstart Trotsky who hadn't even joined the party until 1917.

Kamenev

Zinoviev

Trotsky initially thought he had an ace in the hole: Lenin's last letter. In 1924, he persuaded Lenin's widow to demand its publication. However, Zinoviev was one step ahead of him and made an impassioned speech indicating that the great leader's fears had been unfounded, since the party had prospered so well under Stalin's leadership. Since a majority of the members of the Central Committee had been appointed by Stalin himself, they quickly agreed that Zinoviev was right and the letter remained unpublished.

Heady with the success of once again standing down his old enemy, Stalin moved in for the kill. In 1925, he worked with his allies on the Central Committee to have Trotsky removed from office. Though his supporters urged him to fight the decision, with arms if necessary, Trotsky had had enough of politics and agreed to resign quietly.

Chapter 11: Governor Roosevelt of New York, 1922-1932

Smoothing Relations with Tammany Hall

One of the reasons FDR was so hell bent on finding a cure for his illness was that he understood the permanent damage it might have on his political career. In addition to searching out ways to heal, he maintained a cheerful and sunny demeanor intended to suggest to people that his physical strength was improving. FDR assumed it would bolster his political fortunes.

Despite his 1921 diagnosis, FDR still had his eye cast firmly on his political future. During the early 1920s, he devoted much of his political activities to improving relations with Tammany Hall. Although he had been on the national scene in the Wilson Administration and the vice presidential run, to date the only elected office he had successfully held was a local one representing Hyde Park in the New York State Senate. His home town was a bastion of wealth with no major Irish Catholic or union constituents, but Roosevelt learned in his 1914 failed U.S. Senate run that any Democrat needed the support of Irish Catholics to win statewide office in New York.

Roosevelt thus set out recruiting support from Tammany. His most famous public move in this regard was his two-time support for Al Smith, the first Catholic to be nominated for President. Roosevelt helped Smith win the New York Governorship in 1922 and supported Smith against his cousin, Theodore Roosevelt Jr., in 1924. This move especially was viewed favorably by Tammany Hall. Roosevelt also gave nominating speeches supporting Smith for President in 1924 and 1928, and his 1928 advocacy resulted in Smith's nomination for the Presidency.

Governor of New York

The same year Smith ran for President, the candidate returned Roosevelt's long-standing support by advocating that Roosevelt run to succeed him as Governor of New York. Roosevelt was reluctant to run for Governor and only did so at Smith's urging. Roosevelt still held hopes that he could recover from his paralysis, which he thought limited his ability to succeed politically.

After significant prodding, Roosevelt opted into the race for Governor. He campaigned enthusiastically, but his candidacy was nearly engulfed by rumors that he was too weak to govern. Luckily, his prominence and popularity prevailed, and Roosevelt won the election by a paper-thin margin, with a less than one percent margin of victory over his opponent. This was even more of a success given the national results the Democrats suffered in 1928: Al Smith even lost his home state of New York, and was crushed in his race for the Presidency.

The Beginning of the Depression

Roosevelt's term as Governor coincided with the dawning of the economic catastrophe with which he would be permanently linked. Sworn in in 1929, Governor Roosevelt was confronted by economic depression within months of his inauguration.

While Herbert Hoover attempted without success to fix the economy on a national level, Roosevelt used the Depression to build nationwide stature. He began to advocate a relatively novel idea – that the economy would not fix itself but needed help from government. President Hoover and the Republicans continued to rely on market economics, expecting the economy to end its bust and turn itself around.

Among Roosevelt's major reforms as Governor was the creation of an unemployment relief agency. He also created numerous other social programs aimed at relieving poverty and stimulating the economy, including an old-age pension bill that served as a model for Social Security. Many of these proposals served as precursors for the later New Deal. They, also, however, increased the state's budget deficit, from $15 million when Roosevelt entered office, to $90 million by the time he left.

By 1930, Roosevelt was ready to run for re-election. Unlike in 1928, Roosevelt won reelection by a rousing 14 percentage point margin. This mimicked the national elections, which swept Democrats into House and Senate seats across the country. Due to his initiatives in New York, which were seen as well-thought out policies ahead of the curve, Roosevelt was also positioned as a leading contender for the Democratic Presidential nomination in 1932.

Chapter 12: The Tory Chancellor

As head of the most powerful Department in Whitehall, Churchill proved to be thoroughly traditional in economic outlook. Arguably his most important decision was the 1925 return to the Gold Standard, which in retrospect he regarded as a huge mistake.

The dire economic consequences put downward pressure on wages, which in turn led to a threatened miners' strike and ultimately the nine day General Strike of May 1926. Churchill was fundamentally opposed to the strike, which he regarded as political, in contrast to his more neutral attitude to the underlying miners' dispute, which he viewed as essentially an industrial matter. Baldwin tasked him with editing a daily government mouthpiece, the British Gazette, for the duration of the strike. His forthright views were evident throughout, but the accusation that Churchill had actually provoked the strike, by insisting that the Government abandon talks with the Trade Unions, was not accurate.

He was also constrained by the U.S. administration's attitude to war debt. Great Britain was owed substantially more than it in turn owed to the U.S. Churchill's view at the time was that the slate should be wiped clean across Europe and America, and that to call in the debts would depress economic activity, but it was an argument that he had lost.

Against this bleak backdrop, Chancellor Churchill presented a series of austere budgets, following often difficult discussions with spending departments. He rejected Labour and Liberal calls for major public works to stimulate economic activity and mop up unemployment. In particular, he sought huge defense cuts, especially in the air force and navy. Ironically, as prime minister 15 years later, he would depend upon a reversal of this policy, introduced by Ramsay Macdonald's National government, for Britain's survival.

If this hawkish economic policy was ultimately damaging to Britain, then it certainly did Churchill's reputation within the Conservative Party no harm at all. As the country wrestled with the post war economic challenge, Churchill's traditional medicine, backed by the Bank of England and Treasury officials, convinced most of his party colleagues to set aside their misgivings about his earlier career. Only on the question of free trade was there any serious difference of economic opinion within the party.

Externally of course, there were heavyweight critics. John Maynard Keynes, whose ideology and work were notably revived during debates over how to handle the 21st century's first global recession, famously wrote *The Economic Consequences of Mr Churchill* in 1925 and the press baron Lord Beaverbrook warned him of the risks he ran. In fairness to the Chancellor, he had agonized in particular over the Gold Standard decision. In years to come he was to feel ill-served by his advisors, especially Montagu Norman, Governor of the Bank of England. Keynes was to share this assessment of Churchill's tenure as Chancellor, and there was never any personal rancor between the two.

Keynes

In May 1929 Stanley Baldwin went to the country. The result was a hung parliament, with Ramsay MacDonald forming a minority Labour administration. Churchill, back in favor with many in the party he had deserted in 1904, was also back in opposition.

Chapter 13: 1930s Europe

Stalin's Modernization Programs and Purges

As soon as he no longer needed their help against Trotsky, Stalin began to speak openly against Kamenev and Zinoviev. He attacked Trotsky's position that the role of the Soviet Union should be to spread communism throughout the world, a position also held by Zinoviev and Kamenev. Instead, he maintained that it was more important to solidify and maintain power within the states of the Soviet Union. This put Kamenev and Zinoviev in an awkward position, since they didn't want to oppose a powerful ally and come to agree with a man they had just helped depose.

Since Zinoviev and Kamenev seemed unlikely to continue to support Trotsky, Stalin felt secure enough to turn his political attention to other members of the Central Committee. However, the men soon overcame their embarrassment about their past attacks on Trotsky and finally publically joined forces with him against Stalin in 1926. By that time, however, it was too late and Stalin, accusing them of promoting disharmony and disunity, had them thrown off the Central Committee. Since a political split into a two party system was among the Soviet Union's greatest fears, Zinoviev and Kamenev agreed to resign quietly. Trotsky, on the other hand, made no such promises and was banished to Kazakhstan.

With his political position secured, Stalin turned his attention toward his country's economic situation. In order to make the farms across the Soviet Union produce enough food to feed the ever expanding population, Stalin learned that the farmers would need 250,000 new, gas powered tractors. Not only did these need to be built, but they would need to be powered, so he also had to find a way to pump and refine the extensive oil deposits lying underground in much of the northern regions of the country. Finally, farms needed electricity, which meant more power plants and wires strung across great distances.

In order to accomplish this, Stalin had to get more factories up and running. They had just barely gotten back to their pre-Revolution level of production, much less seen any growth. However, he was determined, and brought the same force that he had already used against the Politburo to bear on the factories. To this end, he created and enforced in 1928 the first of many Five Year Plans.

He began by going after the kulaks. They tended to grow and sell food near their own homes and villages, while he wanted more produce imported into the cities to feed the factory workers and their families. Therefore, in 1928 he began pressuring them to abandon their independent farms and join together as collectives.

Not surprisingly, Stalin's promises of higher production and better profits largely fell on deaf ears. Though he tried to explain that, as part of a cooperative, the farmers could pool their resources and buy better equipment, the men and women who had worked the same land for generations were less than enthusiastic. This did not please Stalin at all, and perhaps even stirred up memories of the peasants who had teased him as a young boy. They definitely stood for all that he had tried to put behind him when he left Gori for the big city.

Frustration often brings out the worst in people, and this was so for Stalin. He ordered his underlings on the local level to take possession of the kulak's land and have them gathered together into state owned collective farms. Those who resisted were shot out right, including thousands of kulak farmers and their families. Furthermore, anyone else who got in his way was sent to Siberia or Russian holdings in Central Asia. According to Soviet records, about 1 in 4 failed to survive the trip.

At the same time Stalin was also determined to see growth in factory output. He set goals for tremendous increases in the production of coal, iron and electricity. He spread rumors that, if these goals were not met, the Soviet Union would be in danger of eminent invasion. He also encouraged factory managers to set high goals for their workers and to publically ostracize those that did not meet them.

Discouraged by insurmountable demands, many workers simply stopped coming in for work. If this became a pattern for an individual, he would be arrested and charged with sabotage by not working hard enough to support the Five Year Plan. If deemed guilty, the worker could be sent to a forced labor camp, either on the dreaded Siberian Railway or along the Baltic Sea Canal. The worst offenders were shot outright as a warning to others.

To be fair, Stalin did not only authorize threats and punishments to motivate workers. He also pushed the Central Committee to offer higher wages to those who excelled. Committee members argued against what they saw as a betrayal of the egalitarian principles of the revolution, but in the end Stalin prevailed, and by the early 1930s those who developed the necessary skills to serve the good of the people could expect to be rewarded with higher wages.

Though his he had won the battle for higher wages, Stalin was in grave danger of losing the war over control of the Politburo. By the summer of 1932, opposition to his policies had risen to such a fevered pitch that members were calling for his expulsion and the reinstatement of Leon Trotsky to power. Not surprisingly, Stalin met this threat aggressively and demanded that those who dared criticize him should be rounded up and shot. At this, even one his staunchest supporters, Sergei Kirov, argued that he had gone too far, and the plan was never executed.

Kirov

By the end of 1932, first Five Year Plan had come to an end and it was time to evaluate its success. In a report to the Politburo, Stalin described the results:

1. The results of the five-year plan have refuted the assertion of the bourgeois and Social-Democratic leaders that the five-year plan was a fantasy, delirium, an unrealizable dream. The results of the five-year plan show that the five-year plan has already been fulfilled.

2. The results of the five-year plan have shattered the well-known bourgeois "article of faith" that the working class is incapable of building the new, that it is capable only of destroying the old. The results of the five-year planhave shown that the working class is just as well able to build the new as to destroy the old.

3. The results of the five-year plan have shattered the thesis of the Social-Democrats that it is impossible to build socialism in one country taken separately. The results of the five-year plan have shown that it is quite possible to build a socialist society in one country; for the economic foundations of such a society have already been laid in the U.S.S.R.

4. The results of the five-year plan have refuted the assertion of bourgeois economists that the capitalist system of economy is the best of all systems, that every other system of economy is unstable and incapable of standing the test of the difficulties of economic development. The results of the five-year plan have shown that the capitalist system of economy is bankrupt and unstable; that it has outlived its day and must give way to another, a higher, Soviet, socialist system of economy; that the only system of economy that has no fear of crises and is able to overcome the difficulties which capitalism cannot solve, is the Soviet system of economy.

5. Finally, the results of the five-year plan have shown that the Communist Party is invincible, if it knows its goal, and if it is not afraid of difficulties.

Of course, Stalin's report failed to mention that despite his collectivization and modernization, famines across the Soviet Union resulted in the deaths of upwards of 5-10 million people. Stalin has been blamed for engineering the Ukrainian famine, to the extent that he has been accused of genocide for the mass starvation.

Hoping to smooth over relations between Stalin and the rest of the party, Kirov suggested in 1934 that Stalin allow those who'd been exiled for opposing him to return home. Stalin did not like this idea, and spent much of that summer trying to persuade Kirov to come back to his way of thinking. Kirov would not agree, however, and was assassinated on December 1 of that year.

Stalin claimed to know nothing of any assassination plot and insisted instead that it was the work of Trotsky and his followers. He had 17 suspects arrested, convicted and executed, including former colleagues Grigory Zinoviev and Lev Kamenev. This was just the beginning, however, and in the years that followed Stalin continued to cleanse the party of those who opposed him. With the help of Nikolai Yezhov, whom he made head of the Communist Secret Police, he saw one member after another arrested, interrogated until they confessed, and executed. By 1938, Stalin had purged so many veteran officials that he felt secure enough to stop the purges, and Yezhov became the fall guy for the excesses of the Great Purge. As a result, Yezhov was forced from his position, and his knowledge of Stalin's Great Purge made him too much of a risk to even try in public, so Yezhov was secretly executed and disposed of in 1940. After his death, Yezhov was very memorably removed from a photo showing him and Stalin, one of the most famous examples of the Soviets' historical revision.

Yezhov

Having purged the government of his enemies, Stalin turned his attention to the Soviet Army. While some historians have argued that Stalin's severe attacks on his fellow countrymen were motivated by nothing more than a paranoid need to solidify power, others maintain that he did indeed have cause for concern. Rumors definitely abounded of coups and attempted coups in the works. However, whether there was any truth behind those rumors remains a mystery.

Whatever his motivation, Stalin showed his usual thorough ruthlessness. In June of 1937 he had eight of his top commanders arrested and charged with conspiracy with Nazi Germany against the Soviet Union. The men were convicted and summarily executed. But this was just the beginning. For the next few years, the Red Army was indeed red, with the blood of 30,000 executed soldiers, including half of all the commissioned officers.

With the government and army thoroughly cleansed of opposition, Stalin attacked the

Communist Secret Police. He appointed a new head, Lavrenti Beria, whom he charged with ferreting out what he called "fascist elements" that he claimed had infiltrated the police force. In reality, it was Baria's job to round up those who knew the details behind the recent killing spree and to see to it that they were silenced. In doing this, he had every leader of the police force executed.

Churchill's Wilderness Years

Churchill later referred to the period between the 1929 election defeat and his return to ministerial office in 1939 as the "Wilderness Years". In truth, what characterized this period for him was that the political positions he took were out of step with mainstream British opinion. Of these, there were three issues which were to define him in the eyes of politicians and the general public: India, the abdication crisis, and Nazi Germany. Of course, his prescience and courage in connection with the latter was to propel him to the highest office, and indeed, into history.

As the dust settled on the general election and Churchill's backstage attempt to build a Liberal-Conservative opposition foundered, he turned away from Westminster, and as he had done in the past when his political options narrowed, he took to travel and writing.

Together with his brother Jack and son Randolph, he made an extensive tour of Canada and the U.S. Traveling mostly by train, and casually flouting the United States' Prohibition laws along the way, he rediscovered a passion for the concept of Anglo-American cooperation - the destiny of the "English speaking peoples". To an extent, it was romantic nonsense, but politically it represented a personal volte-face and the beginning of a conviction which ultimately would enable him to build a relationship with President Franklin Delano Roosevelt that would save the democratic world. Suddenly, Churchill was in favor of an enlarged United States Navy. Staying in New York at the time of the stock market crash, he took it as axiomatic that between them, Britain and America could solve this and almost any other problem.

Back in Britain he continued to develop his ideas and wrote prolifically. However, his sentimental and profligate management of Chartwell soaked up money even faster than he, by now the highest paid writer in the country, could earn it. Fortunately, wealthy friends rallied round. During this period he published *My Early Life* (1930) and began work on the History of the English Speaking Peoples, for which he was paid a handsome advance. He also contributed regularly to the press. In June 1930 he gave the Romanes lecture at Oxford, with a wide-ranging presentation which began to hint at compromise on his long-cherished free trade views, together with economic intervention at home and some fairly radical constitutional proposals. Although out of office, Churchill's political mind never slept, and he never hesitated to call it as he saw it.

For this reason as well, he would not trim or suppress his old fashioned and arguably racist views on the governance of India. The Round Table Conference on the future of India, which reported in 1931, proposed Dominion status that would ultimately imply effective independence, albeit under the crown. All three major political parties, including Churchill's Conservatives, backed the reforms. In this there was early recognition that the pure colonial model was untenable, especially given the articulate, well educated and hugely popular independence movement, led by Mohandas Gandhi. Churchill, grounded in romantic notions of Victorian empire and frankly unconvinced that the Indian people could govern themselves, remained resolutely opposed. Around him gathered 60 or so of the most conservative Conservatives, but the numbers are deceptive: the tide of history had turned and all three party leaders knew it.

Churchill's leadership of the opposition to the 1935 India Bill was colorful and emotional but pointless. It succeeded only in marking him as a man out of touch with modernity. The Bill was passed, but opposition from India's independent princely states, coupled with the advent of World War II, would mean it was never fully implemented as intended. Ultimately India would enjoy full, unfettered independence by 1947. Churchill broke with Baldwin forever and resigned from the shadow cabinet. In December he left for the United States, undertaking a well received lecture tour on his new theme of Anglo-American destiny.

By this time Churchill was equally well established as a critic of the Government's foreign policy, particularly with respect to Germany. His thinking was traditional, calculated British balance of power theory: he saw that an aggressive Germany needed to be checked. Although the Treaty of Versailles that ended the First World War had placed limits on German rearmament, those provisions were routinely being ignored by the Germans, so Britain needed to put the pieces in place on the board in order to do this, with rearmament a priority. Diplomacy from a position of weakness, especially when dealing with a ruthless regime, was pointless. This was a useful counter to some of the wishful thinking and naivety within government circles, but by no means Churchill's only motive. In fact, he was personally appalled at the Nazi regime even by its rise to power in 1933, particularly its anti-semitism. Clement Attlee (the Labour Party leader) recalled Churchill breaking down into tears during a conversation about this before the war[9].

For most of this period, Churchill's criticism of the Government on the question of Germany was measured and constructive, rather than obstinate. It was also well informed - he had contacts in Westminster and Whitehall who supplied him with highly sensitive information. Baldwin's government, formed after the general election of 1935, appointed Churchill to its Air Defense Committee. He was not trusted to join the cabinet, but his acknowledged interest and expertise in air defense would be put to good use.

Churchill spoke out regularly on foreign affairs, but until the Munich crisis his views remained contingent, shaded. Thus he was initially relaxed about Mussolini's Italy, and it was not until halfway through the Spanish Civil War that he sided with the Republican government, setting

---

[9] Quoted in Addison, p140.

aside his distaste for Stalinist Russia and calculating that a Franco-Hitler pact was the more serious threat.

Churchill's intervention in the Abdication Crisis of December of 1936 did nothing to repair relationships with Conservative colleagues. At the time, his critics speculated that he was conspiring to establish a "King's Party" in parliament. But this was 1936, not 1688. Baldwin, most of his government, the Dominions and the British Establishment were appalled by Edward VIII's behavior with Wallace Simpson. There was no question of the King being able to marry Simpson under those circumstances and to remain on the throne. In calling for cooler heads and a delay in taking precipitate action, Churchill was simply acting out of compassion for his friend the King. As was usually the case for Churchill, he simply insisted on speaking his mind. He had a romantic love of the monarchy and a personal liking for the King; he found the idea of abdication distasteful and he wanted to look for an alternative solution. Yet as with his views on India, he was completely out of step with majority opinion.

Although in stressing rearmament he initially enjoyed endorsement from the Conservative right (naturally inclined to support a strong independent Britain), his evolving views tended to keep him at the margins within his party and the country. His advocacy, during the late 1930's, of a multilateral response to Hitler, involving the Popular Front government in France and Stalin's Russia, lost him most Conservative support and gained him few admirers in the Labour Party. The British Left still mistrusted him.

Stalin's Non-Aggression Pact with Hitler

Although Stalin was worried about internal enemies throughout the 1930s, the rest of Europe was preoccupied with the Spanish Civil War and the rise to power of Adolf Hitler and the Nazis in Germany. Seeing this as both an opportunity and a threat, Stalin threw the support of Soviet Russia behind the Popular Front supporting the Spanish Republican government in the Civil War. Not only did he send tanks and aircraft to Spain, but he also sent about 850 personnel to man them and advise the rebels in their fight.

Stalin's main concern, like that of the rest of the world at that time, was Germany. Although the Treaty of Versailles that ended the First World War had placed limits on German rearmament, those provisions were routinely being ignored by the Germans, and European powers thus sensed their own rearmament was a priority. Concerned that Hitler would soon turn his sights on Russia, he began to put out feelers among other European countries about forming an alliance. Initially, his offer was met with skepticism. English Prime Minister Neville Chamberlain disliked Stalin and would have nothing to do his offers. On the other hand, Winston Churchill, who at the time was trying to rally his countrymen to the threat posed by Hitler, saw the practical benefits of the alliance Stalin was offering, saying in a speech May 4, 1938:

"There is no means of maintaining an eastern front against Nazi aggression without the active aid of Russia. Russian interests are deeply concerned in preventing Herr Hitler's designs on Eastern Europe. It should still be possible to range all the States and peoples from the Baltic to the Black Sea in one solid front against a new outrage of invasion. Such a front, if established in good heart, and with resolute and efficient military arrangements, combined with the strength of the Western Powers, may yet confront Hitler, Goering, Himmler, Ribbentrop, Goebbels and co. with forces the German people would be reluctant to challenge."

On 30 September 30 1938, Prime Minister Neville Chamberlain returned to Britain and promised the British "peace for our time", waving a copy of the agreement he had signed with Adolf Hitler and Benito Mussolini in Munich the day before. Of course, Chamberlain and Munich have become synonymous with appeasement, a word that has since taken on very negative connotations, and war would explode across the continent exactly 11 months later.

Chamberlain holds up the Munich Agreement

When Chamberlain visited Hitler in September, Stalin became convinced that England was planning a secret pact with Germany against the Soviet Union. Thus, he decided to try to beat them to the punch. He contacted Hitler and proposed that they form an alliance, going as far as to fire his Commissar of Foreign Affairs, Maxim Litinov, a Jew who was an unacceptable ambassador to Hitler's government. Litinov's replacement met the following month with German foreign minister Joachim von Ribbentrop and on August 28, 1939 they signed the Nazi-

Soviet Pact in which both sides promised to remain neutral in any future war.

From 1936-1939, Hitler took a series of steps in further violation of the Treaty of Versailles, but Europe still refused to confront him. The "appeasement" of Hitler by France and Great Britain before World War II is now roundly condemned, a fact Chamberlain himself came to understand in 1939, noting, "Everything that I have worked for, everything that I have believed in during my public life, has crashed into ruins." Before World War II, however, everyone still had to deal with the haunting specter of the First World War. Thus, most British people were jubilant when Chamberlain returned from Munich in September 1938. They wanted peace, and Churchill was seen as a dangerous warmonger and imperialist who was hopelessly out of touch and out of date.

Hitler

The Beginning of World War II

"History shows that there are no invincible armies and that there never have been." - Stalin

A previous supporter of Chamberlain's (and Churchill had seconded his nomination to lead the Conservative Party when Baldwin resigned in May 1937), Churchill was clear that Britain and France needed to make a stand over Czechoslovakia. He saw Munich as a fundamental error of judgement and an act of political cowardice. It was the result of "five years of futile good intention, five years of eager search for the line of least resistance, five years of uninterrupted retreat of British power[10]", as he told the House on 5th October. His speech represented a complete break with the mainstream Conservative Party. With literally a handful of exceptions, he was without friends in Parliament.

It had been a difficult decade. In Churchill's personal life, the older children had left home, but this was not without its stresses. His son Randolph had caused political embarrassment by standing as an Independent Conservative at a by-election in 1935 without consulting his father. Diana divorced in 1935 after less than three years of marriage, and Sarah's husband Victor Samek was considered "unsuitable" by the family. As 1939 opened and war loomed, Churchill, with difficulties at home and in politics, was truly in the wilderness. He could be forgiven for thinking that this time, he might never come back.

On September 1, 1939, the world was changed forever. Despite several attempts by the French and British to appease Hitler's Nazi regime to avoid war, most notably allowing Hitler to annex the Sudetenland, Germany invaded Poland on that day, officially starting the deadliest conflict in human history. For the French and British, the Nazi invasion of Poland promised war, and by September 3 both countries declared war on Germany. Meanwhile, the Soviet Union, fresh off a nonaggression pact with Hitler, invaded the Baltic. France and the United Kingdom, treating the Soviet attack on Finland as tantamount to entering the war on the side of the Germans, responded to the Soviet invasion by supporting the USSR's expulsion from the League of Nations.

Though Germany was technically Russia's ally, Stalin had no delusions that they were friends. Instead, he used this time to build up his forces for what he saw as an inevitable invasion. First, on the heels of the German invasion of Poland in September 1939, Stalin had his troops invade and reclaim the land Russia had lost in World War I. Next he turned his attention to Finland, which was only 100 miles from the newly named Leningrad. He initially tried to negotiate with the Finnish government for some sort of treaty of mutual support. When this failed he simply invaded. While the giant Russian army ultimately won, the fact that little Finland held them off for three months demonstrated how poorly organized the bigger force was.

Britain and France also began a naval blockade of Germany on September 3 which aimed to damage the country's economy and war effort, but the Nazis would blitzkrieg across the continent over the next year and eventually overwhelm France in mid-1940, leaving the British to fight alone. For the first two years of the war, it looked as though the Axis powers may very well win the war and usher in a new world order.

Chapter 14: President Roosevelt Fights the Depression, 1933 – 1941

---

[10] Hansard, 5th October 1938. Accessed at:http://hansard.millbanksystems.com/commons/1938/oct/05/policy-of-his-majestys-government#S5CV0339P0_19381005_HOC_216 on 8th May 2012 10.00 GMT.

The Election of 1932

With the economy still cratering, Democrats were seething for victory in 1932. The Democrats had only won the White House four times since the Civil War, and each time only because of unusual or precarious circumstances. With the Great Depression deepening, the party saw an opening to shift the American political paradigm in its favor.

Many looked to FDR to carry the banner of change, but not all Democrats were initially convinced. Southern Democrats were especially wary of nominating Roosevelt, ironically because of his supposed pro-Catholic leanings. Roosevelt's early antagonistic relationship with Irish voters in New York belied that belief, and his support of Catholicism had been tepid and political in nature, making it a relatively easy issue for him to surmount. On the fourth ballot at the party's Chicago convention, Roosevelt was selected as the nominee, with Speaker of the House John Nance Garner as his running mate.

Until 1932, tradition dictated that a candidate accept a nomination in writing only. Roosevelt broke this tradition, flew to Chicago, and told the convention "I pledge to you, I pledge to myself, to a new deal for the American people." That phrase would define the first half of his Presidency.

On Election Day, Roosevelt won handily. In one of the biggest margins in electoral history, Roosevelt carried 472 electoral votes to Herbert Hoover's 59, winning 57% of the popular vote to Hoover's 39%. It was an historic victory, indeed. Roosevelt's victory was the first since 1848 in which the Democrats won with a majority of the popular vote, and no President from either party had ever won more electoral votes. Furthermore, the Democrats won substantial majorities in the House and Senate. Thereafter, Democrats would hold a majority in the House for all but four years until 1995. It was, without question, precisely the shift the Democrats had hoped it would be.

By the time Roosevelt was inaugurated in March of 1933, the Depression had worsened. Of the 48 states, 32 had closed their banks due to bank runs, and FDR's inauguration came amid the worst bank run in the history of the Depression, which prompted him to act quickly to counter contagion.

Today, of course, one of the things Roosevelt is most remembered for is his first inaugural address, which understandably addressed the pessimistic mood in the nation. Roosevelt began his speech by saying, "I am certain that my fellow Americans expect that on my induction into the Presidency I will address them with a candor and a decision which the present situation of our Nation impels. This is preeminently the time to speak the truth, the whole truth, frankly and boldly. Nor need we shrink from honestly facing conditions in our country today. This great

Nation will endure as it has endured, will revive and will prosper. So, first of all, let me assert my firm belief that the only thing we have to fear is fear itself—nameless, unreasoning, unjustified terror which paralyzes needed efforts to convert retreat into advance."

Bank Runs

Roosevelt's first 100 Days were unusually active. On his first full day as President, Roosevelt ordered a bank holiday to halt the further run on U.S. banks. He then quickly got to work sending a record number of ideas for bills to Congress, almost all of which were passed easily by the large Democrats majorities in both the House and Senate.

FDR subscribed to a Keynesian view of economics, an outlook that believed the Depression grew worse due to a lack of spending and investment. He thus hoped to stimulate the economy by restoring confidence and offering incentives for people to spend and invest.

On March 9th, just four days after Roosevelt declared a bank holiday, Congress passed the Emergency Banking Act, which required all banks to prove they were solvent before they were able to reopen after the bank holiday. FDR hoped this would allow Americans to be confident that their local bank would not lose their money.

Days later, on March 12th, Roosevelt gave the first of many "Fireside Chats" over radio. The addresses reassured Americans and added to Roosevelt's already-stellar popularity, and they represented a revolutionary way of using new social media by a president.

FDR after one of the "fireside chats"

The First New Deal

From 1933 through 1934, Congress passed the legislation that came to be known as the "First New Deal." New Deal legislation began passing through Congress at the end of March, less than a month into Roosevelt's first term. The first major achievement was the Civilian Conservation Corps (CCC), which put young men between the ages of 18 to 25 to work on a national reforestation program. In mid-April, Roosevelt made an historic move by taking the dollar off the gold standard, thereby giving the Federal Reserve stronger control over the nation's currency.

In May, the Federal Emergency Relief Act was passed, which gave grants rather than loans to states, which allowed them to spend money stimulating their economies. A more controversial act, the Agricultural Adjustment Administration (AAA) passed Congress that same month. The Act paid farmers to NOT till their land, hoping to reduce crop supply, increase prices, and thereby aid ailing farmers in the Heartland.

These initial bills were largely Depression-specific and provided immediate emergency relief. Other bills, however, had a more lasting effect on the economic fabric of the United States. In late May, Congress passed the Federal Securities Act, which required the issuing of stocks and bonds to be registered and approved by the Federal government.

June also brought a flurry of legislative activity. Congress passed the National Industrial Recovery Act (NIRA), the Public Works Administration (PWA), the Farm Credit Act, and the Federal Bank Deposit Insurance Corporation (FDIC), which guaranteed all deposits into insured banks up to a maximum of $2,500. The limit has been increased steadily in each economic crisis since FDR, and was raised to a limit of $250,000 in 2008. Among these pieces of legislation, NIRA was the most controversial. It forced industries to create minimum prices and establish rules of operation within their industry. It also mandated that industries make agreements not to compete. This bill was challenged on legal grounds and would later be found unconstitutional.

Towards the end of 1933, Congress created more Federal jobs programs and ratified the 21st Amendment, ending Prohibition. This was a move heavily favored by Roosevelt's former opponents, the Irish Catholics from the Northeast.

Congress was not finished with the first New Deal in 1933, however. In 1934, it passed the Securities Exchange Act, which established the Securities Exchange Commission (SEC), to clamp down on illegal stock speculation. John F. Kennedy's father, Joseph Kennedy, chaired the Commission. In the same month, Congress passed the Federal Communications Commission (FCC) to regulate radio and telegraphs.

In less than two full years, Franklin Roosevelt achieved more landmark legislative accomplishments than most Presidents had in two terms. He was just getting started.

Supreme Court Resistance to the Second New Deal

The American public was pleased with FDR's actions and awarded him with even larger Democratic majorities in the House and Senate in the 1934 Midterm Elections. However, entering 1935, the First New Deal had only had a small effect on economic recovery: unemployment fell from a high of 25% when Roosevelt was inaugurated to just over 20% by 1935. While it was improvement, the economy was far from bustling again.

In an effort to improve economic conditions, FDR crafted the Second New Deal in an attempt to offer long-term security to the elderly, disabled, unemployed and others in need. The aim of the First New Deal had been merely to stimulate the economy, but the Second New Deal sought to ensure long-term stability.

The Second New Deal was not devoid of stimulus funding, however. One of its first major achievements was the Works Progress Administration (WPA), which employed artists and writers to bring their talents to small towns. More aid was brought to small towns through the Rural Electrification Administration, which brought power to places not served by private companies.

In May of 1935, the Supreme Court dealt FDR's New Deal legislation its first of many defeats when it declared the National Industrial Recovery Act (NIRA) unconstitutional. The following year, it found the Agricultural Adjustment Act unconstitutional as well. During his first term, Roosevelt felt he didn't have a sufficient mandate to take on the court effectively, thus resigning himself to attempting to work around it.

Despite these setbacks, Roosevelt and Congress steamrolled ahead with more major accomplishments. The most important of these were the National Labor Relations Act, the Social Security Act and the Revenue Act.

The Labor Relations Act created the National Labor Relations Board (NLRB), which ensured the right of labor to organize and bargain collectively. This was another piece of legislation influenced heavily by Roosevelt's former opponents in Tammany Hall. The Social Security Act created modern-day Social Security. At the time, it guaranteed a pension for Americans age 65 and over, set up unemployment insurance and assisted states with giving aid to needy citizens, including the disabled.

Apart from reinvigorating the economy, Roosevelt also signed the Neutrality Act in the summer of 1935. The Act prohibited American companies from shipping weapons to belligerents during wartime. Though war had not yet broken out in Europe, Roosevelt's extensive knowledge of the European scene led him to foresee war on the continent.

Winning Reelection and Packing the Court

Roosevelt was reelected in 1936 by an even larger and even more historic margin than he had in 1932. In 1936, President Roosevelt carried every state in the Union except Vermont and Maine, winning 523 electoral votes to his opponent's 8. Roosevelt carried more than 60% of the popular vote, the most of any President in history at the time.

Roosevelt, however, quickly squandered this landmark mandate by taking on the Supreme Court. Frustrated by the Court's opposition to much of his legislation, Roosevelt crafted the Judiciary Reorganization Bill of 1937, which would have allowed him to name an additional Justice for every Justice on the Supreme Court over 70 years old who did not plan to retire within half a year. FDR was very nakedly seeking to remake the court so that it would not continue to overturn important New Deal legislation like NIRA.

Known as Roosevelt's attempt to "pack the court," the proposed legislation was an utter debacle, and it met with strong opposition among considerable segments of the public, the bar, and even Vice President Garner. One editorialist wrote, "[T]hese are not the traits of a democratic leader."

The court packing provisions of the bill were soundly rejected by the Senate and eventually stripped from the bill later in 1937. By that time, the Supreme Court had begun to uphold New Deal legislation on a more frequent basis anyway. And over the course of his entire presidency, Roosevelt was able to appoint 8 new justices to the Supreme Court out of a total of 9 spots.

Focusing on Europe

Foreign policy, a minor part of Roosevelt's first term, came to dominate his second. In December of 1937, Japan attacked the U.S. gunboat *Panay* on China's Yangtze River, even though Roosevelt had already declared neutrality in the war between China and Japan. Japan apologized and said the attack was a case of mistaken identity, but sensing the need for preparation, Congress appropriated $1 billion to upgrade the U.S. Navy in January of 1938.

Throughout 1938 and 1939, war broke out throughout Europe. The social and economic disorder brought about by World War I helped the Nazis rise in Germany. In 1937, Adolf Hitler declared the Treaty of Versailles void and began aggressively annexing parts of the European continent. Europe's attempts to appease him failed, as Nazi Germany swallowed up Austria and Czechoslovakia by 1939. Italy was on the march as well, invading Albania in April of 1939.

During the months and years immediately before the outbreak of war, FDR reiterated America's neutral stance. In May of 1937, another Neutrality Act was passed, now requiring belligerents to pay for non-military U.S. goods in cash and carry them in their own ships. Congress also prohibited the government from loaning money to foreign governments at war.

The straw that broke the camel's back, however, was Germany's invasion of Poland in September of 1939. Two days later, France and Great Britain declared war on Germany and World War II began. This event, and those that followed soonafter, changed Roosevelt's mind. As Assistant Secretary of the Navy in World War I, Roosevelt had wanted the U.S. to involve itself earlier. He didn't feel any differently this time around. Roosevelt thus got to work convincing Americans of the need to support Great Britain in war.

Roosevelt's argument was fueled by Germany's rapid conquest of Poland, Denmark and Norway, and the Battle of Britain, which took place on July 10th, 1940. With these events, Great Britain was essentially on its own fighting Nazi Germany in Europe. The Soviet Union was still abiding by its Nazi-Soviet Non-Aggression Pact, so the USSR was uninvolved. British diplomats began begging the US government for some sort of aid.

Roosevelt initially took small steps. On September 16th, 1940, he signed the Selective Training and Service Act, the first peace-time military draft in US history. All men between the ages of 21 and 35 were required to sign up for the draft.

After winning an unprecedented third term in 1940 – by a significantly smaller, but certainly not narrow, margin than he had previously – Roosevelt began speaking to the American people on the possibility of war in Europe. He framed his arguments in Wilsonian ways, calling the U.S. the last remaining "Arsenal of Democracy." FDR argued that "we are fighting to save a great and precious form of government for ourselves and for the world." He convinced Congress to send aid to Great Britain, on the basis that the US would be defending four essential freedoms. Neutrality was officially over, though war was not yet on.

Chapter 15: Britain Alone, 1940-1

Between the full annexation of Czechoslovakia in May 1939 and Hitler's invasion of Poland in September, considered the official start of World War II, Churchill began to emerge from the political shadows. He had, after all, been vindicated. The Press in particular began to publish positive coverage, and former political enemies began to waver. At the outbreak of war Chamberlain had little choice but to bring him into the War Cabinet - to the Admiralty once more, where it was thought he would be safer with a full operational portfolio.

As with World War I, he was a "hands on" minister. He pushed for the expansion of naval radar, and agitated for British operations in the Baltic. Again, early results were mixed - the loss of the battleship Royal Oak in the supposedly safe haven of Scapa Flow was offset by what Churchill colorfully described as the "superb sea-fight" at the battle of the River Plate.

Characteristically, he was excited by the opportunities offered by a Norwegian campaign. A highly risky proposition, it now seems likely that the German attack in April 1940 which preempted British operations was at least influenced by intelligence Hitler had received. The Germans had suspected that Britain was preparing to make a move. By now Chamberlain had given Churchill chairmanship of the influential Military Coordination Committee. A nervous War Cabinet scaled back some of the more ambitious aspects of the Committee's plan, but nonetheless British, French and Polish troops intervened in Norway that same month. For the most part the campaign was a failure, and as the beaten Allies withdrew. After the debacle there, the decisive Norwegian debate took place in the House of Commons. The collapse in government support at the end of the debate was as much to do with Chamberlain's earlier appeasement than it was to do with Norway per se, which was just as well given Churchill's culpability in the latter.

In any event, a government of national unity was clearly needed. The Labour Party would not support Chamberlain; Halifax (Foreign Secretary and equally one of the appeasers) did not sit in the Commons, which he felt, conveniently perhaps, excluded him from the premiership. That left Churchill as the only credible candidate. As German forces swept into Holland and Belgium on 10th May 1940, Chamberlain advised the King to call for Winston. The complexion of British war leadership was about to change.

Churchill established and energized a new government with cross-party support and a revamped administrative and decision-making apparatus. His deputy was Clement Attlee, leader of the Labour Party. Churchill himself took on the role of Minister of Defense and would exercise personal political control of military strategy for the rest of the war. The Liberal Party was also brought into the Government.

Churchill's routine and leadership style as Prime Minister was eccentric, interventionist, infuriating, grueling, but ultimately and undeniably successful. He would spend much of his morning sitting in bed, reading documents, firing off "Action This Day" memoranda and speaking with senior colleagues by telephone or face to face. From September 1940, his reading would include the latest "Ultra" decrypts from Bletchley Park. The British had cracked the German codes in May, and Churchill wisely insisted on being sent a copy of everything.

After a heavy lunch he would take a nap for an hour or two before chairing a series of meetings, which would usually extend into the evening. He would break for dinner and often watch a film. Then he would work again, with colleagues in attendance, until the early hours. Beginning with white wine at breakfast, alcohol would be consumed throughout.

During the war he enjoyed the active support of his family, all of whom served in one capacity or another. Randolph fought with the specialforces (SAS), parachuted into Yugoslavia and liaised directly with Tito. Wild he might be, but he had his father's courage. Clementine, as well as acting as confidant to her greatly stressed husband, organized charity drives in support of Russia, and his daughters served in the APS and WRVS[11].

As a policy maker Churchill was stubborn, and therefore would nag away at an issue for days or weeks, struggling to get his way. He expected to be challenged and yet he would rarely directly overrule specialist military leaders. Field Marshal Sir Alan Brooke, in particular, described (for example) the battles he fought to prevent a second Allied invasion of Norway. Churchill would dismiss or sideline those whom he considered were not delivering, such as Field Marshal Dill, in 1941. He was sometimes overly attracted to peripheral campaigns, such as the Dodecanese, but at a very strategic level, he had a plan. From the day he took office, he was absolutely determined that Nazi Germany must be beaten, that the means to achieve this was to work for American support, and that in the meantime, Britain would not surrender or compromise. In the dark days of May 1940 that was a clear-sighted and courageous strategy.

Churchill's leadership during 1940 was to become the defining period of his premiership. During the Battle of France, he visited Paris a number of times, in an effort to stiffen French resolve. In a controversial and risky decision, he authorized the despatch of additional RAF fighters to the front, but to no avail. Lord Gort's British Expeditionary Force was evacuated from Dunkirk and the scene was set for French collapse. Fighting a personal battle in cabinet against Chamberlain (still Conservative Party Leader) he would not countenance peace overtures brokered by Mussolini. He promised Parliament, and the nation, nothing but "blood, toil, tears and sweat". In June he ordered the Royal Navy to destroy the French fleet at Oran. This was the pivotal point. It is hard to conceive of any other senior British politician of the day not being tempted to compromise. Britain was alone; but as Admiral Somerville's fleet opened fire on its former allies, it became very clear to the Axis that the war would continue.

---

[11] Auxiliary Territorial Service and Women's Royal Voluntary Service

Picture of the famous evacuation at Dunkirk

Initially, Stalin believed he had several years to build up his army before Germany would invade, figuring it would at least take the Germans that long to conquer France and Britain. However, when France fell quickly in 1940, it seemed he might have miscalculated, so he again sent Molotov to Berlin to stall for time. Meanwhile, Hitler trained his sights on Britain, turning his attention to destroying the Royal Air Force as a pre-requisite for the invasion of Britain. Given how quickly the Nazis had experienced success during the war thus far, perhaps the Luftwaffe's notorious leader, Hermann Goering, was not being entirely unrealistic in 1940 when he boasted, "My Luftwaffe is invincible...And so now we turn to England. How long will this one last - two, three weeks?"

Goering

Goering, of course, was proven wrong. During the desperate air battles that ensued, Britain's investment in radar and modern fighters, coupled with a German switch in tactics, won the day. The Battle of Britain was the only battle of the war fought entirely by air, as the Luftwaffe battled the British Royal Air Force for months during the second half of 1940. The Luftwaffe also bombed British infrastructure and indiscriminately bombed civilian targets, but Germany's attempt to overwhelm the British was repulsed by the Royal Air Force. British cities were targeted, and Churchill's very public tours of wreckage helped make him an icon symbolizing the determined, stubborn resistance of the nation. This was the first real check to Nazi expansionism. Whilst Russia, Greece and others would suffer far more, it was Churchill's defiant and courageous political leadership that made successful resistance seem possible.

The Battle of Britain produced some of the war's most memorable quotes, coming of course from the British prime minister. In reference to the efforts of the Royal Air Force during the Battle of Britain, Churchill famously commended them, stating, "Never…was so much owed by so many to so few.". And as only Churchill could put it, "Their generals told their Prime Minister and his divided Cabinet, 'In three weeks England will have her neck wrung like a chicken.' Some chicken! Some neck!"

Churchill had begun his famous correspondence with President Roosevelt during the autumn of 1939. Although they were not to meet as leaders until August 1941, Churchill spared no effort in stressing the threat to the U.S. from Germany should Britain be defeated and presenting his case in terms of his familiar "English speaking peoples" argument. The relationship was to prove fundamental to the outcome of the war. Roosevelt faced reelection in November 1940 and in any event, isolationist sentiments in the United States ran deep. Against this backdrop, the Destroyers for Bases deal in September 1940 was above all a political triumph for Churchill - as he saw it, inching the Americans towards intervention.

Domestically, 1940 allowed him to strengthen his grip on the government. Chamberlain retired, sick, in September. Churchill wisely secured the party leadership for himself - not difficult under the circumstances. Halifax was moved to the embassy in Washington, allowing Churchill to bring his old ally Eden into the government as Home Secretary. The "Guilty Men" of Munich were gone.

Militarily, the winter of 1940-41 saw the Italians ejected from East Africa and a stunning offensive into Libya in December, under the command of General Richard O'Conner. Although Italy had attacked on both fronts earlier in 1940, it was clear that her forces were completely outmatched by the British. As had already been seen in France however, fighting toe to toe with the Wehrmacht was a different proposition.

In March 1941, Germany invaded Greece and Yugoslavia in an effort to shore up her right flank prior to attacking Russia. Italy had already become mired in a war with Greece along the border with Albania. In a decision which remains open to criticism, Churchill pressured Wavell, in command in the Mediterranean, to send a force to Greece. Militarily this was a huge gamble, and it failed to pay off. The result was another costly evacuation, the loss of Crete, and a weakened army in North Africa, which was quickly pushed back by a newly arrived German armored corps under Rommel. It was not that Churchill or those around him were blind to these risks. Rather, as Max Hastings writes, the British decision was driven by "an overriding moral imperative"[12]. If no aid was to be provided to an ally attacked by Nazi Germany - then what was the war being fought for?

---

[12] Hastings, e-book location 2216.

Rommel, the Desert Fox

Operation Barbarossa

Stalin knew that if he could delay an invasion through the summer of 1941, he would be safe for another year. Unfortunately for Stalin, Molotov's mission failed and Hitler began to plan to invade Russia on May 15, 1941. Since military secrets are typically the hardest to keep, Stalin soon began to hear rumors of the invasion. However, when Prime Minister of England Winston Churchill contacted him in April of 1941 warning him that German troops seemed to be massing on Russia's border, Stalin remained dubious.

Stalin felt even more secure in his position when the Germans failed to invade the following May. What he did not realize was that Hitler had simply over stretched himself in Yugoslavia and only planned to delay the invasion by a few weeks. Hitler aimed to destroy Stalin's Communist regime, but he also hoped to gain access to resources in Russia, particularly oil. Throughout the first half of 1941, Germany dug in to safeguard against an Allied invasion of Western Europe as it began to mobilize millions of troops to invade the Soviet Union. Stalin even refused to believe the report of a German defector who claimed that the troops were massing on the Soviet border at that very moment.

On June 22, 1941, Stalin had to admit he was wrong; 3,400 German tanks and three million soldiers rolled across the Russian border and headed toward Leningrad, commencing Operation

Barbarossa. The Soviets were so caught by surprise that the Germans were able to push several hundred miles into Russia across a front that stretched dozens of miles long, reaching the major cities of Leningrad and Sevastopol in just three months.

The first major Russian city in their path was Minsk, which fell in only six days. In order to make clear his determination to win at all costs, Stalin had the three men in charge of the troops defending Minsk executed for their failure to hold their position. This move, along with unspeakable atrocities by the German soldiers against the people of Minsk, solidified the Soviet will. In the future, Russian soldiers would fight to the death rather than surrender, and in July, Stalin exhorted the nation, "It is time to finish retreating. Not one step back! Such should now be our main slogan. ... Henceforth the solid law of discipline for each commander, Red Army soldier, and commissar should be the requirement — not a single step back without order from higher command."

Certainly their resolve was tried during the first terrible months of fighting, as Germany surrounded Leningrad and then headed toward Moscow. The worst fighting, however, was in the Ukraine. Though badly outnumbered and destined for defeat, the Soviet soldiers held off the Germans around Kiev and thus spared Moscow while it was reinforced. They suffered the worst defeat in Red Army history, but were praised as heroes by their countrymen.

In September, as winter months approached, Germany continued to advance across the countryside. This led Stalin to implement his famous "scorched earth" policy, ordering the retreating soldiers to leave nothing behind that the advancing Germans might be able to use. He also approved the formation of small bands of guerilla fighters who would remain behind the retreating army and harass the advancing German forces. These two strategies, along with Germany's ever thinning supply line, created quite a handicap for Hitler's army.

To his credit, Stalin took a page out the Royal Family of England's book and remained in Moscow even when the city was evacuated and the Germans were only fifteen miles away. He lived and worked in a bomb shelter just under the Kremlin, acting as self-appointed Supreme Commander-in-Chief and overseeing every move made by the army. He bided his time and waited until November, when the German army was forced by bad weather to end their forward movements.

The Germans had reached the vital resource centers in Russia that they were aiming for, but the sheer size of Russia had enabled the Soviet Union to mobilize millions more to fight, requiring the Germans to dig in and prepare for long term sieges, even while the notoriously harsh Russian winter was setting in.

After Hitler invaded Russia, Britain supplied the Soviet Union with immediate military aid. Again, the substance may prove marginal and the cost high, but here was another state attacked by Germany. Something had to be done. As ever, the overriding priority remained - the defeat of Germany.

Pearl Harbor

On January 20th, 1941, Roosevelt became the first President to be inaugurated for a third term, and much like his first swearing-in, his third inauguration came amidst a major crisis. War was ravaging Europe, with Nazi Germany conquering much of the continent. In response, the US gradually shifted from its neutral stance. In March, Roosevelt signed the Lend-Lease Act, which authorized the President to give arms to any nation if it was in US national interest. With this Act, the US was able to support Great Britain without declaring war on Nazi Germany or Italy.

By the summer of 1941, U.S. entry into the war seemed just on the horizon. Germany violated the Nazi-Soviet Pact and invaded the Soviet Union, spreading war to virtually every piece of the European continent. President Roosevelt and Prime Minister Winston Churchill (another powerful distant relative) met secretly off the coast of Canada in August. The two issued the Atlantic Charter, a statement of Allied goals in the war. It largely reiterated Wilsonian rights, but also specified that a US/UK victory would not lead to territorial expansion or punitive punishment.

However, a substantial segment of the American public did not appreciate the more bellicose direction President Roosevelt seemed to be heading toward. Before the "Greatest Generation" saved Western Europe, many of them were part of the largest anti-war organization in the country's history. In 1940, the United States was still mired in the Great Depression, with nearly 8,000,000 Americans still unemployed, but World War II was the most controversial issue in politics. As the Nazis raced across Western Europe in the first year of the war, young students formed the "America First Committee" in Chicago, an isolationist group supported by future presidents Gerald Ford and John F. Kennedy. The isolationist group aimed to keep the country out of European wars and focus on building America's defenses.

The group expanded to include hundreds of thousands of members by 1941, staunchly opposing President Roosevelt's "Lend-Lease" act, which helped arm the Allies. The America First Committee remained popular and powerful until the morning of December 7, 1941.

Pearl Harbor in October 1941

Once the Germans invaded the Soviet Union, the Japanese no longer needed to worry about their border with Russia, allowing them to focus exclusively on expanding across the Far East and various islands in the Pacific. Though the Japanese steadily expanded across the Pacific theater during 1941, they were running low on vital resources, including metal and oil. In response to Japanese aggression in China and other places, the United States had imposed a crippling embargo on Japan, exacerbating their problem. Moreover, by winter of 1941, the most obvious target for Japanese expansion was the Phillipines, held by American forces.

Ironically, because both sides anticipated the potential for war in 1941, they each made key decisions that brought about the attack on Pearl Harbor. Watching Japan's expansion, the United States moved to protect the Phillipines, leading President Roosevelt to station a majority of the Pacific fleet at Pearl Harbor. Japan, assuming that aggression toward British targets and the Dutch East Indies would bring the United States into the war, decided they had to inflict a blow to the United States that would set back its war effort long enough to ensure Japanese access to resources.

Japan plotted and trained for an attack on Pearl Harbor for several months leading up to December 7. Believing that a successful attack on the Pacific fleet would buy Japan enough time to win the war, the Japanese decided to focus their attack exclusively on battleships, ignoring infrastructure on the Hawaiian islands. The Japanese also knew American aircraft carriers would not be at Pearl Harbor but decided to proceed anyway.

All Americans are now familiar with the "day that will live in infamy." On December 7, 1941, the Japanese conducted a surprise attack against the naval base at Pearl Harbor (called Hawaii Operation or Operation AI by the Japanese Imperial General Headquarters). The attack was intended to keep the U.S. Pacific Fleet from interfering with Japan's military actions in Southeast Asia.

The attacks took American forces completely by surprise, inflicting massive damage to the Pacific fleet and nearly 3,000 American casualties. Several battleships were sunk in the attack. Shortly after the attacks ended, the Japanese formally delivered a letter to the United States ending negotiations. Hours later, the Japanese invaded the Phillipines, where American military leaders had anticipated a surprise attack before Pearl Harbor. Even still, the Japanese quickly overran the Phillipines.

Roosevelt giving his famous speech on December 8, 1941

Roosevelt addressed Congress and the nation the following day, giving a stirring speech seeking a declaration of war against Japan. The beginning lines of the speech are instantly familiar, with Roosevelt forever marking Pearl Harbor in the national conscience as "a date which will live in infamy." Of course, the America First Committee instantly became a thing of the past, and the United States began fully mobilizing almost overnight, thanks to the peacetime draft Roosevelt had implemented. The bill helped the country's armed forces swell by two million within months of Pearl Harbor. In 1942 alone, six million men headed off to North Africa, Great Britain and the Pacific Ocean, carrying weapons in one hand and pictures of pin-up models like Betty Grable in the other. Japanese Admiral Hara Tadaichi would later comment, "We won a great tactical victory at Pearl Harbor and thereby lost the war."

Roosevelt signs the declaration of war against Japan

Chapter 16: Turning the Tide, 1942

"We won a great tactical victory at Pearl Harbor and thereby lost the war." – Admiral Hara Tadaichi

Within a month of war, Roosevelt ordered all foreigners in the United States of German, Italian or Japanese origin to register with the U.S. government, a controversially preemptive step that clearly suspected these ethnic Americans of disloyalty. In February, FDR took it a step further by forcing all Japanese-Americans on the West Coast be moved into internment camps throughout the West. This devastated the Japanese-American community, as well as Asian-Americans of other nationalities who were mistaken for being Japanese. Many Chinese and Koreans were interned alongside Japanese-Americans in the West.

The Japanese attack on Pearl Harbor had truly globalized the war, but with American entry into the war it also convinced Churchill that the Allies would win. He initiated a grueling program of worldwide shuttle diplomacy, rightly recognizing the need for top level coordination in order to defeat the Axis powers as swiftly as possible. Whether traveling by battleship or specially conditioned aircraft, this was a punishing regime for a man of his age. With him would be his doctor, his closest advisors, and other senior politicians and military commanders as appropriate. In December 1943 he developed a life-threatening case of pneumonia, not helped by his consumption of alcohol and Cuban cigars, but even then he refused to be bedridden for long.

The string of conferences that Churchill attended would witness an initial convergence of Anglo-American ideas, followed by tensions over the launching of a second front, and culminating in the problem of dealing with the Soviet threat at Yalta and Potsdam. The flux and flow of great armies and fleets across the globe would in no small measure, be governed by this dialogue.

Churchill began from a position of strength, wowing Congress and the Canadian Parliament in December 1941, and securing commitment to a "Europe First" strategy at the Arcadia conference. At the start of 1942, Americans badly wanted to avenge Pearl Harbor, but the British and Soviet Union also had different war priorities. In 1941, the Germans and British were fighting in North Africa, and Churchill wanted help there, with General Montgomery fighting the legendary "Desert Fox," General Rommel. On the other hand, the Soviets badly wanted immediate help on the continent, which would force Hitler to pull away troops in Russia. The Allied leaders had important decisions to make.

Ultimately, President Roosevelt had considerable empathy for the leader of the nation which had been fighting Germany alone since 1940 and which was now also confronting Japan in the Pacific. Churchill's emotional oratory played on this, and again he stressed the "English speaking peoples" theme. The Anglo-American alliance did not only address immediate questions of military strategy: the Atlantic Charter first signed in the summer of 1941 fed directly into Allied war aims, and Roosevelt's concept of the "United Nations", first articulated at Arcadia, was the forerunner of the post-war system of international governance. In June, Britain and the U.S. pooled their atomic research, all of which became the backbone of the Manhattan Project.

The fact that British and American forces were suffering large defeats at the hands of Japan did not matter in the long term. But it presented immediate political difficulties for Churchill. In Asia, Britain lost two of its most powerful warships - sunk in a 20 minute attack by Japanese naval aircraft. Hong Kong also fell. But most devastating was the surrender of 130,000 British and Commonwealth troops at Singapore - arguably the worst defeat in British military history. In

Europe, the bungled raid on Dieppe in August 1942 may have taught the British important amphibious lessons, but it had the feel of another Gallipoli or Norway.

Churchill blamed himself for Singapore, accepting the widely held view that the island had not been properly fortified. Certainly he had opposed investment in its defenses during the '20s. The truth was worse: Commonwealth troops had been poorly led and completely outfought by the tactically superior and much smaller Japanese army. In the desert, Tobruk had fallen and the Eighth Army pushed back to El Alamein. His consequent decision to fly to Cairo and sack Auchinleck was ruthless and political. Auchinleck had proven his worth by stopping the Axis advance. His replacement, Montgomery, would successfully counter-attack in October, but only when safely re-supplied with hundreds of American-built tanks.

In fact, the reverses had caused rumblings at home. Sir Stafford Cripps, like Churchill a maverick but from the Left, was naively advocating a closer alliance with the Soviet Union. The Times of London and other newspapers were calling Churchill's leadership into question. Ultimately, it was Montgomery's victory at second El Alamein and the shrewd promotion of Cripps to the War Cabinet that served to head off most of these problems. The battle at El Alamein induced the Germans to quit North Africa, which paved the way for an Allied invasion of Italy in 1943.

For its part, the United States began 1942 determined to avenge Pearl Harbor, but the Allies, now including the Soviet Union by necessity, did not agree on the war strategy. In 1941, both the Germans and British moved armies into North Africa, where Italy had already tried and failed to reach the Suez Canal. The British sought American help in North Africa, where British General Montgomery was fighting the legendary "Desert Fox," General Erwin Rommel. At the same time, Stalin was desperate for Allied action on the European continent that could free up the pressure on the besieged Soviets. Roosevelt eventually sided with Churchill and decided to land American forces on North Africa to assist the British against Rommel, much to Stalin's chagrin. While the Americans and British could merely harass the Germans with air power and naval forces in the Atlantic, Stalin's Red Army had to take Hitler's best shots in Russia throughout 1942. But the Red Army's tenuous hold continued to cripple the Nazi war machine while buying the other Allies precious time.

Despite fighting in North Africa and the Atlantic, the United States still had the resources and manpower to fight the Japanese in the Pacific. Though the Japanese had crippled the American fleet at Pearl Harbor, its distance from Japan made an invasion of Pearl Harbor impossible, and Japan had not severely damaged important infrastructure. Thus, the United States was able to quickly rebuild a fleet, still stationed at Pearl Harbor right in the heart of the Pacific. This forward location allowed the United States to immediately push deeply into the Pacific theater.

In fact, the turning point in the Pacific theater took place in 1942 near Midway Island. The Japanese had moved a sizable fleet intending to occupy Midway Island and draw the American navy near. Instead, American aircraft flying from three aircraft carriers that had been away from Pearl Harbor in December 1941 got a bearing on the Japanese fleet and sunk four Japanese aircraft carriers, permanently crippling Japan's navy. The Battle of Midway was the first naval battle in history where the enemy fleets never saw or came into contact with each other. Thus, 1942 ended with the United States turning the tide in the Pacific and North Africa, giving the Allies momentum entering 1943.

General Montgomery

The Eastern Front

Even before 1942, Stalin ordered a general attack, ordering the Soviet army to throw everything it had against the Germans beginning on December 4th, 1941. The German army was caught off guard and soon driven back 200 miles. For the rest of the war, Stalin would be known for his orders to attack, attack and attack again. Because of this aggressive strategy, he was always in need of fresh troops, but it became easier to recruit willing soldiers as he demonstrated the German army was not the invincible monster everyone had feared. In fact, the Russian army's tenacity eventually became an inspiration for all the allied armies opposing Hitler.

Unfortunately, once Old General Winter withdrew his troops in the spring of 1942, Germany once more made inroads toward Stalingrad, Stalin's own pet city. Not surprisingly, he ordered that it be held no matter what. There was more than vanity at stake though. Stalingrad was all that stood between Hitler and Moscow. It also was the last major obstacle to the Russian oil fields in the Caucuses which Stalin needed and Hitler coveted. If the city fell, so would the rest of the country—and Hitler would have an invaluable resource to fuel his armies.

Stalin chose his best general, Marshal Georgy Zhukov, to lead the more than one million soldiers who would stand between Germany and the precious city. Stalin made sure that they were continually supplied with every sort of military paraphernalia available, from tanks and aircraft to guns and ammunition. He also took this opportunity to point out that his prophesy on the importance of industrialization to national security was finally proving true. Had there not been so many factories turning out weapons, the city would never have been held.

Zhukov

Zhukov, who had never been defeated, held the line until November 19, when Stalin ordered him to attack the now weary Germans. In a carefully planned pincer maneuver, the Soviet armies attacked from both the north and the south, carefully encircling the German troops until the German general, Friedrich Paulus, begged Hitler to allow him to withdraw. But by then the Fuhrer was obsessed with capturing the city that he refused his general's pleas, so the Germans attempted to hold on, losing thousands of additional men without taking the city. When Paulus surrendered on January 30, he had lost 1.5 million men and over 6,000 tanks and aircraft.

Chapter 17: 1943

From January 14th to the 24th of 1943, Roosevelt, Churchill and other allied leaders met in Casablanca, Morocco. The Casablanca Conference set out Allies demands for an unconditional surrender of Axis Powers. The leaders also agreed to the first major allied assault on Europe: an invasion from North Africa via Sicily into Germany. Roosevelt also agreed to increase submarine bombing in the Atlantic and to send more aid to the Soviet Union.

Entering 1943, the Allies looked to press their advantage in the Pacific and Western Europe. The United States was firmly pushing the Japanese back across the Pacific, while the Americans and British plotted a major invasion somewhere in Western Europe to relieve the pressure on the Soviets, who had just lifted the siege of Stalingrad. The Allies were now firmly winning the war. From January 14th to the 24th of 1943, Roosevelt, Churchill and other Allied leaders met in Casablanca, Morocco, but Stalin declined so that he could stay back and manage affairs in Stalingrad. The Casablanca Conference set out Allies demands for an unconditional surrender of Axis Powers. The leaders also agreed to the first major allied assault on Europe: an invasion from North Africa via Sicily into Germany. Roosevelt also agreed to increase submarine bombing in the Atlantic and to send more aid to the Soviet Union

The Allies now had the potential to invade Western Europe or even use North Africa from which to launch an invasion, meaning the Germans had to prepare for several contingencies. And despite fighting in North Africa and the Atlantic, the United States still had the manpower and resources to cripple the Japanese at the Battle of Midway, the first naval battle ever fought in which both navies were never in sight of each other. For their part, the Russians had destroyed an entire German army at Stalingrad by February 1943, and Hitler's Russian invasion had passed its apex.

Stalingrad proved to be Germany's high water-mark against the Soviet Union. For the rest of the war, they were in a constant state of retreat. As the Red Army chased them out and retook more and more of the countryside, they were appalled by the treatment both soldiers and civilians had received at the German's hands. Over four million Soviet prisoners of war had died of starvation, sickness and other forms of mistreatment. In continuation of the "Final Solution," they had also killed all the Jews they captured, as well as civilians of any other ethnic group Hitler didn't care for. It seems that their thought process was that the more Soviet people they killed, the fewer they'd have to deal with later. It has been estimated that the invading Nazis completely razed over 10,000 Russian villages to the ground, slaughtering all the inhabitants they could get their hands on.

As word of German genocide spread throughout the Soviet Union it had a galvanizing rather than weakening effect. Instead of surrendering to the invading forces in hopes of receiving fair treatment, the Soviet peasants would hide in the woods when they heard of an approaching German army. From there, they would organize guerrilla groups that would strike at the Germans from all angles, picking off sentries, disrupting supply lines and spreading chaos. Likewise, the Russian soldier knew that he had a better chance of survival in the field of battle than if they were taken prisoner, so they were more than willing to fight to the death.

Following the victory at Stalingrad, Stalin was gratified to be invited to join Churchill and Franklin Delano Roosevelt at a secret conference in Teheran in November 1943. Once ostracized by the now disgraced Chamberlain, Stalin must have felt vindicated as he sat down as a member of "The Big Three." However, his pleasure was short lived as Churchill and Roosevelt once more denied his request that the allies immediately open up a second front to drive the Germans out of Western Europe. Unfortunately Stalin's own success at Stalingrad had demonstrated that England and the United States were not as necessary to Soviet survival as Stalin had once claimed.

The British and Americans debated over their next course of action, with the British favoring an invasion of Sicily over the skepticism of the Americans, who believed the operation was overly ambitious and not a direct enough strike against Hitler's Germany. Eventually the British won out by arguing that invading and controlling Sicily would give the Allies a free hand across the Mediterranean Sea, facilitating both commerce and transportation. Since the invasion would be made by the 7th U.S. Army (led by Patton) and the British 8th Army (led by Montgomery), the soldiers in the North African theater, the operation fell under the overall command of Eisenhower.

In July 1943, less than half a year after the surrender at Stalingrad, the Allies conducted what at the time was the largest amphibious invasion in history, coordinating the landing of two whole armies on Sicily over a front more than 100 miles long. Within a month, the Allies had taken control of the entire island, setting in motion a chain of events that led to Italy quitting the war and Mussolini being hanged. Though Italy was no longer fighting for the Axis, German forces continued to occupy and control Italy in 1943. The Germans attempted to resist the Allies' invasion on Sicily but were badly outmanned and outgunned, leading to a German evacuation of the island within a month. The Allies would land on the mainland of Italy in September and continue to campaign against the Germans there.

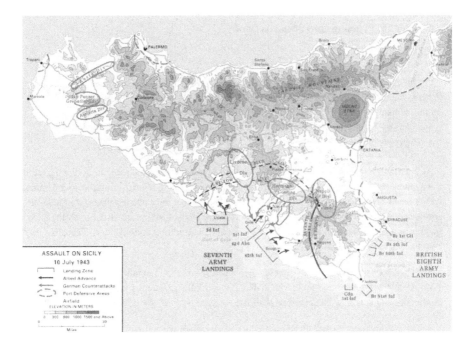

Stalingrad proved to be Germany's high water-mark against the Soviet Union. For the rest of the war, they were in a constant state of retreat. As the Red Army chased them out and retook more and more of the countryside, they were appalled by the treatment both soldiers and civilians had received at the German's hands. Over four million Soviet prisoners of war had died of starvation, sickness and other forms of mistreatment. In continuation of the "Final Solution," they had also killed all the Jews they captured, as well as civilians of any other ethnic group Hitler didn't care for. It seems that their thought process was that the more Soviet people they killed, the fewer they'd have to deal with later. It has been estimated that the invading Nazis completely razed over 10,000 Russian villages to the ground, slaughtering all the inhabitants they could get their hands on.

As word of German genocide spread throughout the Soviet Union it had a galvanizing rather than weakening effect. Instead of surrendering to the invading forces in hopes of receiving fair treatment, the Soviet peasants would hide in the woods when they heard of an approaching German army. From there, they would organize guerrilla groups that would strike at the Germans from all angles, picking off sentries, disrupting supply lines and spreading chaos. Likewise, the Russian soldier knew that he had a better chance of survival in the field of battle than if they were taken prisoner, so they were more than willing to fight to the death.

Chapter 18: Planning Operation Overlord

Buildup and Deception

For the Allied leaders, the main strategic issue became that of the so called Second Front. Where would the main effort of the Western Allies be in 1944? The first tensions with Roosevelt on this subject arose in Quebec, in August 1943. It had been hard work to convince the Americans of the merits of an invasion of Sicily. Now Churchill was sure that an Italian campaign was the key to defeating Germany.

At Tehran in November 1943, Stalin was at a disadvantage. He was something like the out of town stranger that someone had brought home for Thanksgiving Dinner. England and America were related both ethnically and politically. They also spoke the same language, ate the same sorts of foods and shared a mutual history going back nearly 1,000 years. Russia, on the other hand, was a mystery, a separate entity steeped in archaic tradition and mystery. Therefore, Stalin could not help but feel like an outsider.

Still, Stalin had no problem holding his own when it came time to talk of military strategy. Lord Alan Brooke, a British Field Marshall and Churchill's aid, kept a lengthy diary of the conference. This is how he described Stalin:

> "During this meeting and all the subsequent ones which we had with Stalin, I rapidly grew to appreciate the fact that he had a military brain of the very highest calibre. Never once in any of his statements did he make any strategic error, nor did he ever fail to appreciate all the implications of a situation with a quick and unerring eye. In this respect he stood out compared with his two colleagues."

Ultimately, Stalin sided with Roosevelt and pressured the British into accepting a cross-channel invasion of France for the following year. Churchill was reluctantly forced to recognize that Britain had become the junior partner in the enterprise.

Strategically, Churchill's Mediterranean obsession was questionable. Indeed, his insistence that Britain should go it alone during the failed Dodecanese campaign of September-November 1943 represents his stubbornness at its worst. The Italian campaign was prosecuted, but it had quickly stagnated into precisely the kind of slugging match that Churchill had feared in France. His argument that this failure should be reinforced was rightly rejected by Roosevelt and his advisors. Even the outflanking maneuver at Anzio faltered within a week, with superior German leadership able to seal off the beach-head before the Allies could seize Rome.

Still, Churchill's views were partially understandable. Seeking battle in the obvious critical sector tends to lead to attritional warfare, as Grant found during the Overland Campaign of the American Civil War in 1864-5. It works if the attackers have an overwhelming preponderance, but Britain was desperately short of troops. A large-scale invasion across the channel seemed to represent a big gamble with all of the chips down.

Churchill disagreed with the planning of Operation Overlord, but he lost his argument. Though the Allies used misinformation to try deceiving the Germans, all sides understood that the most sensible place for an invasion logistically was across the English Channel. The Germans had constructed the Atlantic Wall, a network of coastal fortifications throughout France, to defend against just this kind of invasion. Thus, the Allies devised an extremely complex amphibious attack that would be precipitated by naval and air bombardment, paratroopers, and even inflatable tanks that would be able to fire on fortifications from the coastline, all while landing nearly 150,000 men across nearly 70 miles of French beaches. The Allies would then use their beachhead to create an artificial dock, eventually planning to land nearly 1 million men in France.

During the first half of 1944, the Americans and British began a massive buildup of men and resources in the United Kingdom, while Eisenhower and the military leaders devised an enormous and complex amphibious invasion of Western Europe. Though the Allies theoretically had several different staging grounds for an attack on different sides of the continent, the most obvious place for an invasion was just across the English Channel from Britain into France. And though the Allies used misinformation to deceive the Germans, Hitler's men built an extensive network of coastal fortifications throughout France to protect against just such an invasion.

Largely under the supervision of Rommel, the Germans constructed the "Atlantic Wall", across which reinforced concrete pillboxes for German defenders were built close to the beaches for infantry to use machine guns and anti-tank artillery. Large obstacles were placed along the beaches to effectively block tanks on the ground, while mines and underwater obstacles were planted to stop landing craft from getting close enough.

The Green Line marks the Atlantic Wall

A pillbox

The Atlantic Wall necessitated an elaborate and complex invasion plan that would ensure the men who landed wouldn't be fish in a barrel. Thus, the Allies began drawing up an elaborate battle plan that would include naval and air bombardment, paratroopers, and even inflatable tanks that would be able to fire on fortifications from the coastline, all while landing over 150,000 men across 50 miles of French beaches. And that was just the beginning; the Allies intended to create a beachhead that could support an artificially constructed dock, after which nearly 1 million men would be ferried to France for the final push of the war.

Throughout the first half of 1944, France, once a lightly defended area used largely for the recuperation of German soldiers from the Eastern front, was now the focus of Allied and German attention, with feverish plans made for the region on both sides. Reinforcements flooded into Northern France while tacticians planned for the impending invasion and counter-attack. The speed with which Germany had reinforced and strengthened the region meant that the Allies were less than certain of the success of the invasion. Britain, weary of amphibious landings after the disastrous Expeditionary Force campaign of 1940 came perilously close complete obliteration, was more than anxious. Allied military fortunes had been, at best, mixed. Professor

Newton points out Britain, together with its continental allies, had lost its foothold in Europe but had managed to bloody the nose of Germany in the Battle of Britain in the summer of 1940. The Allies had lost Crete, yet stopped the Afrika Corps at El Alamein. With its American allies, Britain had successfully invaded Italy before becoming entangled in the costly German defense of the country. Britain, as a small island nation, lacked the manpower and supplies needed to singlehandedly defeat the German military. In comparison, the United States, an industrial colossus, had ample men and materials. Like Britain, American fortunes in the European theater were mixed, ranging from the successful landings in North Africa to the debacle of Kasserine Pass.

A sense of fear and foreboding marred the weeks and months in the build up to the invasion. Churchill was aghast at Eisenhower's bombing plan to accompany the landings, which would have resulted in the deaths of between 80,000 and 150,000 French civilians. It would have been an outrageous number of civilian casualties, and more French citizens killed by Allied bombing than had lost their lives in four years of German occupation. Churchill felt it was better to continue the bombing of Germany rather than inflict terrible casualties upon their French allies in support of what may be a doomed invasion. Just months before the planned invasion of France, Allied forces had landed at Anzio, just south of Rome. Almost immediately, the Allied landing force was halted and almost driven back into the sea. Churchill himself had been a leading player in the invasion of Gallipoli in 1915, a debacle which almost cost him his career. The idea of landing on the heavily defended Normandy coast filled Churchill with fear. On one occasion, just weeks before the launch of *Overlord,* the Prime Minister was heard to say, ""Why are we doing this? Why do we not land instead in a friendly territory, the territory of our oldest ally? Why do we not land in Portugal?"

Churchill was not alone. Many of the British military planners had felt a cross channel invasion "smacked of a seaborne Somme". Churchill had, however, persuaded the U.S. to give priority to the war in Europe, a position which caused many difficulties for Roosevelt. Pearl Harbor had outraged America and inflamed popular opinion against Japan, yet American attitudes towards Germany and Italy were far more ambivalent, due to the large proportion of American citizens with German or Italian heritage. However, at the somewhat bizarre Rattle Conference, described as a combination of intensive study and a 1920s themed house party, organised by Lord Louis Mountbatten, the assembled company settled upon Normandy as the invasion destination. Although further from Germany, it offered the Allies the chance to capture two major ports, Cherbourg and Le Harve.

The Allies relied upon deception as a force multiplier. Churchill particularly understood the importance of deception, when at the "Big Three" Conference he said, "In wartime, truth is so precious that she should always be attended by a bodyguard of lies." The resulting *Operation Bodyguard* was the deception plan created for use with the Normandy invasion. The plan was to trick the Germans into thinking the expected invasion would come in late summer 1944, and would be accompanied by an invasion in Norway, Greece and elsewhere in Europe. The goal was to trick the Germans into defending areas away from the invasion, thus posing less threat to the success of *Overlord*. On an operational level it hoped to disguise the strength, timing and objectives of the invasion.

A further element of *Bodyguard* was *Operation Fortitude*. *Fortitude* marked one of the most ambitious, successful deception plans in the history of warfare. *Fortitude* was divided into two parts, North and South. Both parts involved the creation of fake armies, one based in Edinburgh in the north and one on the south east coast of England which threatened Pas de Calais, the most obvious area of France for invasion. The Allies went to remarkable lengths to ensure the success of the operation. A fictional U.S. Army group under George Patton was created in the south. Every effort was made to ensure operational security while also allowing the Germans to see the dummy war material and supporting infrastructure to add weight to the ruse. Dummy invasion craft were constructed at ports, inflatable trucks and tanks lined the roads in Scotland and around Patton's fictional army group. Luftwaffe aircraft were allowed fly over the inflatable army while being kept far from the actual invasion preparations. The deception was reinforced by frantic radio signals emanating from *Fortitude* north and south to the amount expected from a large size invasion group.

Inflatable British tank as part of *Operation Bodyguard*.

A crucial factor to the success of Allied deception was the use of double agents. Successful espionage by Mi-5 had turned all German agents in Britain to the Allied side by the launch of *Overlord*. By the beginning of 1944, Mi-5 had 15 agents feeding false information to the

Germans, with just enough reliable information to maintain their credibility. The most celebrated was 'Garbo', a Spanish agent who created a fictitious network of 24 spies while working as a double agent for the British. The benefits of having such a fictitious network of sub agents was Garbo could create an identity for his sub agents to best fit the information given to the Germans.

British Double Agent Garbo

Ensuring the Germans took the bait was a far more difficult prospect than creating the misinformation in the first instance. By 1944, the Allies had a massive advantage in terms of intelligence with the cracking of German enigma codes. Allied deciphering of German codes was so successful by 1944 that those responsible literally could not keep up with the overflow of information. What the intelligence was showing was that the Germans, in the days preceding the invasion of Europe, still had no real idea when or where the invasion was to take place. To complement the allied deception effort, the Royal Air Force dropped twice as many bombs on the Pas de Calais than it did in Normandy in preparation for the invasion. The operation's success can be seen in the length of time it took the Germans to realize it was deception, even after the landings of June 6. It was not until mid-July that the German High Command realized Patton's threat to Calais from southern England was over. Without *Fortitude*, the Germans would have had free reign to maximise its forces at the point of attack in Normandy and with it, it is unclear whether the Allied invasion would have succeeded. Against such a formidable foe, however, the Allies needed to rely on every trick in the book.

The Final Planning

Upon his appointment as Supreme Allied Commander in January 1944, Eisenhower wasted little time in demanding the scale of the landings be increased from three divisions to five. This step had far reaching ramifications in terms of resources and transport. Extra landing craft, support vessels, mine sweepers and bombardment vessels would be needed in a hurry to match the expansion of the invasion plans. Luckily, the U.S. forces were able to muster the extra ships needed.

In the early spring of 1944, the final stages of the planning took shape. Landings would occur at five separate beaches in divisional strength. Prior to this, Beach Reconnaissance Parties were covertly landed at the five sites on dark nights to ascertain the nature, defences and gradients of the beaches. The day before the invasion, D-Day -1, Allied minesweepers would have to be visible to the German defenses in order to complete their duties successfully. Either due to bad weather, German withdrawals or poor patrolling, the minesweepers were not detected.

In the early hours of the morning of June 4, the decision of which day to launch the invasion was made upon the advice of meteorologists. In the days before the decision to launch, the weather approaching the Normandy beaches had been the worst for years, so bad that a landing would be all but impossible. Landings could be undertaken for just 10 days per month due to the tides and the need for a full moon to aid navigation. Delaying the landings in the early part of June would have meant that another attempt could not have been made for at least two weeks, and with well over 150,000 troops already on their ships waiting to go, that situation was not acceptable. Luckily for the Allies, chief meteorologist, Captain Stagg, with the aid of a meteorological station on the west coast of Ireland, was able to inform the assembled commanders that a brief clearing in the weather for a number of hours looked likely.

Ramsay, head of Naval affairs, informed Eisenhower that the Royal Navy would do whatever was asked of it, Montgomery, commander of the ground forces favored immediate action, while Leigh-Mallory, commander of the air-fleet was hesitant, worried that the bad weather would limit the support his air force could give to the landing troops. After a brief pause of no more than a few seconds, Eisenhower simply said "Let's go". With that, the largest invasion fleet ever assembled began its journey towards the Normandy coast. On June 5, 1944, an armada of some 7,000 ships began to cross the Channel towards the Normandy peninsula. Above it, 1,400 troop transports and 11,590 military aircraft of various types (along with 3,700 fighters) supported the landings. The following day, 175,000 soldiers would attempt to land on French beaches.

Even with that horde, to say the Allies faced a daunting task would be an understatement. On the morning of June 6, 1944, General Eisenhower was carrying a letter in his coat that apologized for the failure of the operation. Found years after D-Day, Eisenhower's letter read, *"Our landings in the Cherbourg-Havre area have failed to gain a satisfactory foothold and I have withdrawn the troops. My decision to attack at this time and place was based on the best information available. The troops, the air and the Navy did all that bravery and devotion to duty could do. If any blame or fault attaches to the attempt, it is mine alone."*

General Eisenhower

Chapter 19: D-Day & Operation Overlord

Storming Omaha Beach

From the very beginning of June 6, 1944, events did not go as the Allies had planned. In the first operations of the day, a cloud of Allied aircraft flew overhead, targeting German troop concentrations, infrastructure and fortifications throughout the Normandy countryside. On D-Day alone, Allied air forces flew over 14,000 sorties, compared to just 100 for the Luftwaffe, a clear sign of the total superiority the Allies enjoyed.

The Allied airborne assault in the early morning hours of June 6, 1944 proved to be as full of complexity, drama, heroism, confusion, loss and effort as the beach landings that followed. However, despite the heroism, the airborne assaults did not go to plan. The Allies' planes mostly missed German fortifications on their bombing runs, and tens of thousands of paratroopers who were to land directly behind German lines were dropped out of place due to poor visibility. The only true advantage the paratrooper drops had for the Allies was that the scattered nature of the paratroopers confused the German defenders.

Meanwhile, the span of the amphibious landings that morning covered an area of 55 miles, a length large enough for the Allies to ensure a funnel of resupply could be held. The British had been eyeing up France's coastline and had prepared ingenius armored vehicles to assist the landings. Under the command of Major-General Percy Hobart, flame-throwing tanks, flail tanks to clear mines and bridging equipment, mockingly known as Hobart's "funnies", proved to be a monumental success on the British landing beaches. Omar Bradley, the U.S. commander of ground forces was, unfortunately for his troops, uninterested in such machines. American troops were forced to cross the killing zones and minefields unaided by the new inventions.

Due to the reinforced German positions and heavy artillery pieces with which the Allies faced, the British laid on a two hour bombardment before attempting a landing. Unfortunately for the U.S. forces, particularly on Omaha, Bradley felt a 20 minute bombardment would be sufficient, relying on the Army Air Force to launch a massive attack. But such an attack had been made impossible for the Air Force due to the low cloud cover that had resulted in bombers entirely missing the German positions below. Bradley further compounded the impending misery and torment for his ground troops by completely disregarding the advice of Major-General Pete Corlett, a veteran of successful Pacific amphibious landings. Bradley's attitude was far from open minded and dismissed Corlett's advice by saying "anything that happened in the Pacific was strictly bush-league stuff."

Bradley's decision not to employ adequate naval bombardment robbed his troops of crucial support. For example, a Brooklyn type cruiser, as was available to Bradley on D-Day, could fire 1,500 five inch shells in ten minutes, and when directed by spotter aircraft, its fire was deadly accurate. Yet Bradley, with his deep suspicion and prejudices against the U.S. Navy, remained ignorant. Nevertheless, and to the relief of the U.S. troops at Omaha, when it became obvious the landings there were teetering on failure, a number of destroyer skippers moved their vessels so close to the shore that they risked beaching to support the hard-pressed troops.

In the narrative of D-Day, Omaha Beach has become the best known part of the attacks among Americans, due to the various difficulties the Americans faced there before managing to succeed. But it's essential to remember that each of the 5 beaches were their own story, and largely forgotten is the remarkable success of the the American landings at Utah Beach, which were easier in comparison to the other four landing zones. On Utah, the 4th Infantry suffered only 197 casualties out of a total landing force of 23,000 men.

If the landings at Utah could be described as easy, those at Omaha were chronically bad. Due to the aforementioned failure to reinforce Omaha Beach, despite Rommel's insistence, the U.S. Army encountered just two battalions, rather than the ten which should have been in position. Those two divisions, however, were more than enough to guarantee the U.S. Army one of its worst days in history.

Despite the fact the Germans had just two battalions in position, the landings at Omaha were a disaster. Some military operations are dogged by bad luck, and Omaha is certainly one of those. To begin with, the initial air bombardment completely missed its intended target, and the naval bombardment of just 20 minutes hardly damaged any German defenses. General Bradley had told his men, "You men should consider yourself lucky. You are going to have ringside seats for the greatest show on earth." However, Rear Admiral John L. Hall, in reference to the lack of naval bombardment, countered, "It's a crime to send me on the biggest amphibious attack in history with such inadequate naval gunfire support.

Bradley

Things went wrong even before troops hit Omaha Beach, but inadequacies in naval and air bombardment weren't the only problems. The invasion called for deploying inflatable tanks on the water that could provide cover for the infantry, but the officer in charge of releasing the amphibious tanks panicked and sent them into the deep swells of the Channel, causing 29 of the 34 tanks immediately sinking to the bottom. Finally, since the landing came at low tide, the troops were forced to move across 300 yards of water, followed by 100 yards of beach, steep dunes, and finally swamp, minefield and barbed wire. If a soldier had managed to run the gauntlet and survive, he then faced a climb up the cliffs to the high ground.

The result was, unsurprisingly, a slaughter. Much of the first wave of troops was gunned down before they could get out of the water. Machine gun and rifle fire pinned down those landing craft not destroyed by underwater mines, while those pinned down in the dunes, many gravely injured, were in no position to return any meaningful fire. After these first landing vehicles kept landing along a narrow strip unsheltered against the German defenders, similar landings were suspended during the morning hours of the operation.

Only the ingenuity of the on-looking destroyer captains, who risked beaching their craft to aid the unfortunate troops, provided some relief. Before sun had set on June 6, over 2,500 U.S.

troops were dead, with some units incurring up to 95% casualties. Only thanks to the efforts of low ranking officers and NCOs did the U.S. avoid complete annihilation on Omaha. Pressing through the unimaginable fire, a few managed to begin clearing German defences.

Omaha Beach on the afternoon of D-Day

Recovering the dead at Omaha.

By the end of D-Day, troops on Omaha had only managed to grab two small beachheads, isolated from each other no less, making it the least successful landing spot among the five beaches. It would take a few more days for the Allies to firmly consolidate its hold on Omaha Beach and begin to push inland, after which a MULBERRY harbor was placed there. Somewhat fittingly, the harbor experienced the worst storms in the area in decades, and three days of storms irreparably wrecked the harbor on June 22.

Nevertheless, the preciously bought beach became the main supply zone for the invasion of France. Over the next three months, the Allies used Omaha Beach to land a million tons of supplies, 100,000 vehicles, and 600,000 men, while evacuating nearly 100,000 casualties.

Using Omaha Beach after D-Day

The aims of the British landings at Gold were to establish a link between the British and the U.S. forces at Omaha. Due in part to the heavy naval bombardment of Gold Beach, the British forces were able to overrun the German defences in most places, although they suffered heavy losses in attacks on German strong points such as Le Hamel. For the British it was a success, but certainly not a smooth, unopposed ride as the following quote shows: "We hit two mines going in…They didn't stop us, although the ramp was damaged and an officer standing on it was killed. The first man off was a commando sergeant in full kit. He disappeared like a stone into six feet of water. The beach was strewn with wreckage, a blazing tank, bundles of blankets and kit, bodies and bits of bodies. One bloke near me was blown in half and his lower half collapsed in a bloody heap on the sand."

Like other sectors, Gold Beach did not go entirely according to plan, mostly because the tidal waters that day left the water levels higher than planned. Engineers who were meant to remove some of the obstacles found that British ships were passing over them, which was helpful in some ways and harmful in others. As a contingency, the amphibious tanks had to be landed on the beach, providing necessary cover for the infantry.

After about 3 hours, the British had successfully established a beachhead on Gold Beach. The British division was able to advance through the suburbs of the town of Bayeux after penetrating the German defences, one of the few Norman cities to fall without a fight. Of the 25,000 men who landed on Gold Beach, only about 400 became casualties. "Hobart's Funnies", which had been the subject of ridicule, proved invaluable at Gold Beach, with the different modified tanks clearing minefields, briding ditches, and creating trackways across the sands to facilitate movement on and off the beaches.

By the end of D-Day, the British soldiers who landed on Gold Beach were about 6 miles inland, allowing them to link up with the Canadians on Juno Beach. Moreover, the success at Gold was crucial to the embattled U.S. Army on Omaha, because it drew German fighters away from the struggling Americans.

The 3rd Canadian Division landing at Juno Beach experienced much of the same success as the British, albeit with higher casualties. Due to the Canadians arriving late on the beach, the tide was high, ensuring Rommel's underwater mines were able to inflict as much damage as possible. No fewer than 20 of the 24 lead landing craft were damaged or destroyed. The German army also managed to put up stern defenses around Juno.

Like the British however, the Canadians had the foresight to land their amphibious tanks on the beach when circumstances required it. With the help of these tanks providing cover, the Canadians were able to flank the German defenders, breaching the strong outer layer of German defenses relatively quickly in the northern section of the beach.

The Canadian soldiers landing in the south had it worse. As the 8th Brigade's reserve battalion, Le Régiment de la Chaudière, headed to shore, mines badly damaged their landing crafts, and the soldiers lost almost all of their supplies swimming to shore. With Canadian units pinned down in the south, reserves that landed less than an hour after the initial attacks found to their horror that the German strongholds defending their sector had not been reduced. The 400 man No. 48 (Royal Marine) Commando lost nearly 200 men within seconds of landing.

Despite suffering a total of about 1,000 casualties, the Canadians were able to pour through and push inland. German forces were unable to mount a counterattack until the brutal, murderous Waffen SS Hitlerjugend arrived the following day. By then, the Canadians were well positioned enough to absorb and survive the vicious counterattack. While they received heavy casualties, killed, wounded and captured, with many of the captured brutally murdered by the SS, the Canadians held their ground and pressed on towards the main provincial town of Caen.

The Sword landings were, in comparison to those at Juno, quite easy. Generally, the heavy naval bombardment quelled German resistance, except the heavily defended stronghold of La Breche, which held on for up to three hours. The men on Sword Beach were the only ones to face a determined German counterattack, which came from the 21st Panzer division. But air superiority and effective defenses ensured that the German counterattack almost entirely fizzled out, and the Germans that made progress were eventually compelled to retreat by the end of the day anyway.

Still, two main problems confronted the British attackers. As British forces piled onto the beach, those at the front struggled to break through some German lines, creating a backlog on the beach that left some of the British wide open to indiscriminate German artillery, which inflicted significant loss of life and panic. The 3rd British Division, after landing on Sword, was tasked with meeting up with the British Airborne, which had taken the strategically important Pegasus Bridge in one of the few airborne operations that was successful on D-Day. From there, the British units were to move south towards Caen, eventually linking up with the British and Canadians landing on Gold and Juno Beaches.

However, with British forces massing outside Caen, the plan began to go wrong. Due to the congestion on Sword Beach, the supporting armor was unable to reach the infantry further south. Further compounding the British problem, the heavily defended Hillman fortress stood directly in their path. A particularly bloody and drawn out battle ensued which lasted for most of the afternoon. As British troops pushed towards Caen they encountered elements of the 21st Panzer Division, ensuring Caen would not fall until the middle of July. Considering the varying degrees of success on all the landing beaches, it is perhaps a blessing in disguise that the taking of Caen was delayed, as it allowed Allied forces to better coordinate their attack against the well defended city.

By the end of D-Day, the Allies had managed to successfully land 170,000 men: over 75,000 on the British and Canadian beaches, 57,000 on the American beaches, and over 24,000 airborne troops. Thanks to Allied deception, the German army had failed to react to prevent the Allies from making the most of their landings. Just one division, the Hitlerjugend, would arrive the following day. Despite a fearsome and bloody day, the majority of the Allied forces had held their nerve, and most importantly, achieved their objectives. This ensured *Operation Overlord* was ultimately successful, and victory in Europe would be achieved within less than a year.

Churchill was not overstating the achievements of *Operation Overlord* when he described the plan "the greatest thing we have ever attempted". On D-Day, the greatest armada the world had ever seen had landed 170,000 soldiers on the heavily defended beaches of Normandy in just 24 hours. More remarkable was the fact that the operation was a success on every major level. Deception, tactical surprise and overwhelming force had contributed to the establishment of an adequate beachhead. Confusion and dissent had stopped the Germans massing for any great counterattack. The Atlantic Wall which Hitler had placed so much faith in had been breached, and the race to Paris was on.

Operation Overlord aimed to have the Allies reach the Seine River within 3 months of D-Day, and it's a testament to the men who fought and served on D-Day that the goal was reached early.

To do so, the Allies overcame firm resistance from the Germans, atrocious weather that limited resupply for the Allies, and the difficult terrain of Normandy, which included endless hedgerows providing hidden cover. And the Allies reached their objective ahead of time despite the fact the objectives of D-Day were not entirely met; the Allies had not captured Caen, St-lo or Bayeux on the first day.

Nevertheless, the landings were clearly a resounding success. Casualties were significantly smaller than those expected by commanders, and the significance of D-Day to the morale of the Western world, much of it under German domination, cannot be underestimated. For France, Poland, Czechoslovakia, Belgium, Holland and more, who had suffered over four years of occupation, the great democracies were finally coming to their rescue. American, British, Canadian, Polish, Commonwealth, Greek, Belgian, Dutch and Norwegian soldiers, sailors, and airmen all participated in the Battle for Normandy, which saw the Allies on the banks of the Seine River just 80 days after D-Day.

24 hours after the landings on June 6, 1944, however, the Allies still had plenty of work to do, and when the Allied High Command assessed the situation on the ground, it was clear that on no front had all of the objectives been achieved. The British and Canadians were ashore on Gold, Juno and Sword, yet Caen lay firmly in German hands. And in most cases, the various invasion forces lay clustered in isolated bands.

Nevertheless, the breakout after D-Day went smoothly, and by the end of August, Paris had been liberated and the German Army in France was shattered, with 200,000 killed or wounded and a further 200,000 captured. Hitler reacted to the news of invasion in a fashion which illustrates why Germany lost the war. He welcomed it with glee, figuring it would give the Germans a chance to destroy the Allied armies that had water to their backs. "The news couldn't be better" he said, "we have them where we can destroy them." Hitler's delusion in June 1944, as well as his misplaced faith in the strength of his Atlantic Wall, all helped contribute to the Germans' defeat in Normandy. At no stage were adequate reinforcements released or even contemplated in time to stem the tide of the Allies' momentum.

Paris would be liberated in August, and the Allies would reach the Seine less by December, less than 3 months after D-Day. The end of the war was in sight.

Chapter 20: The End of World War II

Redrawing Europe

Sensing victory, the Allies began planning for a post-war world in the months after D-Day. In July 1944, diplomats from 44 nations come together in Bretton Woods, New Hampshire, where they established the International Monetary Fund (IMF). Otherwise known as the World Bank, the organization was aimed at providing funds for reconstructing countries devastated by war. The following month, the U.S., Great Britain, China and the USSR met at the Dumbarton Oaks Conference to begin planning the formation of a stronger League of Nations, this time to be called the United Nations.

After D-Day had all but sealed the Allied victory, Stalin's Red Army became more aggressive in retaking land formerly held by Germany. Concerned over the ever widening Soviet map, Churchill met with Stalin in October of 1944 (Roosevelt was by this time too frail to join them) and, while ceding Rumania and Bulgaria to the Soviets, insisted that Yugoslavia and Hungary be shared among the allies. The sticking point, however, was Poland. Stalin demanded that the very anti-communist Polish government in exile be overturned in favor of a one more sympathetic to his regime. Churchill, on the other hand, felt a sense of obligation to the government as it stood, since they were hiding out in London. However, he wisely agreed to table the subject until the end of the war was clearly in sight.

At that bilateral meeting, Churchill purported to divide the post war European states up proportionately, in terms of British and Soviet influence. Bulgaria would be 75% Soviet, for example. Stalin appeared to agree, but this was naive nonsense. Not only did it ignore Britain's diminishing role, but it was hard to envision how democratic Britain could share influence with an expansionist Soviet dictatorship within one given state. This scheme would ultimately be vetoed by the Americans, in an episode which further undermined Churchill's relationship with Roosevelt. Yet Stalin's apparent "acceptance" of Britain's suppression of the Greek communists in December 1944, seemed to accord with the deal and certainly led Churchill to trust him more than he should have done when they met with Roosevelt at Yalta.

With the war coming to a gradual end, Roosevelt sought a remarkable fourth term as President of the United States. Roosevelt was the first to receive a third term, but also became the first to receive an astounding fourth term when he was reelected in November. The election of 1944 was his narrowest margin, though it was still a healthy victory. Roosevelt received 432 electoral votes to Thomas Dewey's 99. Roosevelt won 36 of the 48 states, and managed to surmount the Republican argument that no President should remain in office for 16 years. Harry Truman was elected to serve as Roosevelt's third Vice President.

On the home front, Roosevelt also pondered the effects of an end to war on the U.S. economy. Military mobilization had offered a huge boom to the domestic economy, but would an end to that boom put a clamp on economic growth and bring back depression? Congress and the President thus passed the Servicemen's Readjustment Act, which offered free medical treatment, low-interest loans on homes and a free education to returning servicemen. Known as the G.I. Bill, the law later allowed over 20 million soldiers to go to college, expanded home ownership more than ever before in U.S. history, and ushered in the boom years of the 1950's. Thanks to these steps, a post-war recession was avoided.

As the defeat of Germany became obvious and imminent, the future of Europe began to dominate the Big Three's thinking. Controversially, Churchill distanced himself from the Allied campaign of bombing German cities after the Dresden firestorm in early 1945. Churchill figured Britain might need Germany after the war, and he believed there was little point in further embittering its population and destroying its industrial base. He had countenanced and resourced the morally questionable bombing policy since its inception. Yet now, having seen footage of the results, he was not so sure. Whilst Churchill's maneuvering on this issue looked like betrayal to Air Chief Marshall Harris, two points are worth making: a) this was not 1942 - the war against Germany was being won by troops on the ground; b) when Harris and Churchill had initiated the policy it was the only means Britain had at striking at Germany - his own scientific advisor had told him that bombing alone would knock Germany out of the war. Plus there was the undeniable moral question, which nagged away at him.

More strategically, Churchill and Roosevelt worried about Russia. What was to become of Eastern Europe, Poland especially? For his own part, Churchill's conduct on this issue veered from one extreme to another. Militarily, he went as far as to instruct Montgomery to begin stockpiling captured German weapons in 1945, with a view to rearming the Wehrmacht and marching eastwards. Back in London his military planners drew up a feasibility study, but everyone had to concede it was most certainly not feasible. Politically, Churchill probably knew that the Russians would have all the cards in their hand and that therefore, his only hope was to strike a personal deal with Stalin. He was arrogant enough to believe that his charm could outweigh Stalin's cunning and the facts on the ground represented by Russian divisions.

The three leaders at Yalta

The Yalta Conference

The Yalta Conference took place in February 1945, at a time when the Allies were pushing the Nazis back on both fronts and it was clear the war in Europe was ending. The Big 3 held the conference with the intention of redrawing the postwar map, but within a few years, the Cold War divided the continent. As a result, Yalta became a subject of intense controversy, and to some extent, it has remained controversial. Among the agreements, the Conference called for Germany's unconditional surrender, the split of Berlin, and German demilitarization and reparations. Stalin, Churchill and Roosevelt also discussed the status of Poland, and Russian involvement in the United Nations.

By this time Stalin had thoroughly established Soviet authority in most of Eastern Europe and made it clear that he had no intention of giving up lands his soldiers had fought and died for.

The best he would offer Churchill and Roosevelt was the promise that he would allow free elections to be held. He made it clear, though, that the only acceptable outcome to any Polish election would be one that supported communism. One Allied negotiator would later describe Stalin's very formidable negotiating skills. "Marshal Stalin as a negotiator was the toughest proposition of all. Indeed, after something like thirty years' experience of international conferences of one kind and another, if I had to pick a team for going into a conference room, Stalin would be my first choice. Of course the man was ruthless and of course he knew his purpose. He never wasted a word. He never stormed, he was seldom even irritated."

The final question lay in what to do with a conquered Germany. Both the Western Allies and Stalin wanted Berlin, and knew that whoever held the most of it when the truce was signed would end up controlling the city. Thus they spent the next several months pushing their generals further and further toward this goal, but the Russians got there first. Thus, when the victorious allies met in Potsdam in 1945, it remained Britain and America's task to convince Stalin to divide the country, and even the city, between them. They accomplished this, but at a terrible cost: Russia got liberated Austria.

While Roosevelt and later Truman were very concerned about the post-war Soviet Union, Russian undertakings at Yalta, particularly with respect to Poland, were accepted by Churchill at face value. During the subsequent parliamentary debate, comparisons were made with the debacle that transpired at Munich only six years earlier. Yet it would have been impossible for Churchill to publicly disown the deal: doing so would have snuffed out the possibility, however remote, that some kind of pluralism would be tolerated in Soviet-occupied Poland.

Roosevelt's Death

As it turned out, Yalta was also to be Roosevelt's last big conference. Roosevelt was exhausted after the Yalta Conference. Many, including FDR himself, thought the lull in the war allowed the stress of the previous years to finally catch up with him. To relax, Roosevelt went to the spas of Warm Springs, Georgia, where he had spent much time attempting to recover from paralysis after attracting polio. While sitting for a presidential portrait painting, Roosevelt complained of sudden headaches. Hours later, on April 12th, 1945, still sitting for the portrait, Roosevelt slumped forward and died of a massive stroke, less than a month before victory would be achieved in Europe.

When Roosevelt died, he was with his life-long mistress, Lucy Mercer. The two had carried on an affair throughout FDR's presidency. Secret Service Agents escorted Mercer away when Eleanor Roosevelt was brought in to see her husband's body.

Roosevelt's death was met with shock in the U.S. and around the world. Though his health had been declining, and he seemed out of it at times at Yalta, the public knew little about his illness.

He was 63 at the time of death.

Roosevelt's funeral procession down Pennsylvania Avenue

Churchill did not attend the funeral. He may well have been too busy to cross the Atlantic, but critics have suggested that there was an element of sour grapes in the decision.

Germany and Japan Surrender

On April 30, Hitler committed suicide, and Germany surrendered on May 7. By the time of the Potsdam conference in July 1945, Germany had been defeated, and though he didn't yet know it, so had Churchill. The other parties in his National government had insisted on a general election without waiting for the outcome of the war against Japan, although after the deadly Okinawa campaign, it was only a matter of when Japan would be defeated. He therefore ran a Conservative-only "caretaker" administration from May until July.

Though the countries had often discussed Russia joining America and Britain's fight against the Japanese, it became clear at Potsdam that this was not going to happen. Instead, Stalin pleaded for help for his own country, which had been decimated by the fighting with Germany. Russia had lost more than 30,000 factories and so much farm land that the vast majority of the population was suffering from malnutrition. However, he failed to get much of a sympathetic hearing from Truman who, unlike his predecessor, was not particularly interested in the global picture.

Stalin was, however, and he was particularly concerned that the Allies might stage an invasion of Russia and overthrow his regime. While it may have seemed at the time that he was just being paranoid, we now know that George Patton was already pushing Truman and the other world leaders to go ahead and finish the weakened Soviets off. Thus, Stalin was actually wise to build up Communist governments in Czechoslovakia, East Germany, Bulgaria and elsewhere.

The British and Americans didn't see it that way, though. Instead, they assumed that Stalin was expanding the Soviet Union in preparation for invading Europe. The Europeans appealed to the Americans for help and with them created the North Atlantic Treaty Organization in 1949. This mutual mistrust among all parties involved marked the beginning of the Cold War.

During the election, Churchill campaigned on his war record, without sufficient emphasis on the future welfare of the British public. He also launched paranoid attacks on the Labour Party, claiming they would introduce a "gestapo" in Britain. The irony was that a major report advocating a comprehensive system of social security had been prepared by one of his own government ministers - the Liberal William Beveridge. Though he had been one of the most radical social reformers of the early 20th century, Churchill's support for the Beveridge report was lukewarm. In the end the Conservative party did support it, but he did not use this to neutralize a Labour opposition which was advocating the transformation of Britain with evangelical zeal. That was what a war-weary public wanted to hear, and what they voted for. It is hard to blame Churchill for neglecting domestic policy during the war years, but the price he eventually paid was overwhelming defeat at the polls.

Churchill had taken Attlee to Potsdam on the sound democratic basis that the votes were still being counted (this was a lengthy process with so many serving overseas), and that nobody could pre-judge the result. He was nonetheless, deeply shocked. He submitted his resignation to the King on 26th July 1945 and Attlee completed the British negotiations at Potsdam. Churchill, in accordance with his 1942 accord with Roosevelt, had already assented to the use of atomic weapons against Japan. When he left office, the war had only three weeks left.

Vice President Harry Truman, somewhat unprepared for the Presidency, now had to fill some of the biggest shoes in American history. Incredibly, Truman had not been informed of the country's secret attempt to build atomic bombs. Now, faced with the prospect of having to invade Japan and suffering staggering casualties, Truman decided to drop an atomic bomb on Hiroshima on August 6, 1945. When Japan did not surrender, the Americans dropped another atomic bomb on Nagasaki on August 9, 1945. Unbeknownst to the Japanese, the United States had used all the atomic bombs they currently had, and it would take weeks to use another one.

World War II was so horrific that in its aftermath, the victorious Allies sought to address every aspect of it to both punish war criminals and attempt to ensure that there was never a conflict like it again. World War II was unprecedented in terms of the global scale of the fighting, the number of both civilian and military casualties, the practice of total war, and war crimes. World War II also left two undisputed, ideologically opposed superpowers standing, shaping global politics over the last 65 years. As a result, World War II's legacies are still strongly felt today. In the wake of the war, the European continent was devastated, leaving the Soviet Union and the United States as uncontested superpowers. This ushered in over 45 years of the Cold War, and a political alignment of Western democracies against the Communist Soviet bloc that literally split Berlin in two.

Chapter 21: The Cold War

The Berlin Airlift

At the end of World War II, Stalin hoped to continue to expand Soviet influence by blockading West Berlin, which was occupied by France, the United Kingdom and the United States. After the war, Germany had been split up into four parts, one part for each of the four major Allies, and though Berlin was in the Soviet Union's sector, it was also split four ways. The Western allies therefore had an enclave in West Berlin that was totally surrounded by communist territory, and Stalin then ordered a blockade of all supplies into West Berlin, hoping the other Allies would cede the city to the Soviet sector of Germany.

However, the United States and its allies were able to organize a massive airlift of supplies that kept the city of West Berlin supplied. Over the next 11 months, between June 1948 and May 1949 England, America and several other western European countries delivered thousands of tons of food and fuel to the city. The Soviet Union and its German allies eventually stopped the blockade when they realized the West could continue to supply Berlin by air indefinitely. As a result of their heroic efforts, West Berlin survived and Stalin was beaten.

The Korean War

Stalin's next great mistake involved Korea. Korea had been occupied by Japan and was ceded to the Allies after World War II. Without taking into consideration the fact that he had ordered his Soviet representative to the United Nations to withdraw, he persuaded North Korean dictator Kim il-Sung to invade South Korea. In 1950, communist Korean forces, with communist Chinese and Soviet support, invaded South Korea, which was supported by the West. The communist forces hoped to occupy all of Korea and make it a communist state

When the U.N. voted to send troops to oppose the spread of communism, there was not a Soviet representative present to exercise the country's veto power in the Security Council. The resulting war lasted over three years, and saw the United States military fighting communist forces in battle for the first time. The western forces almost captured the entire Korean peninsula until the communist Chinese entered the war. After much fighting, the two sides agreed on a cease-fire line at the original border at the 38th parallel. The cease-fire line created the border between western ally South Korea and communist North Korea.

Although the Russians were indirectly involved in the Korean War, the important result of the Korean War was that the Red Scare spread like wild fire through the United States, deteriorating U.S.-Soviet relations to an all-time low. In the decade that followed, it would become clear to the world that power was no longer divided among many little countries in the world but instead rested almost exclusively in the hands of the U.S. and the USSR. The Korean War was also the first eample of America's containment strategy, which sought to protect non-communist nations from communist aggression to prevent the spread of communism to other countries. Containment would remain the primary American foreign policy strategy for decades.

The Beginnings of the Space Race

When World War II was over, the United States and Soviet Union turned their attention from Nazi Germany to each other. Both sides began secretly working to recruit the Nazi scientists involved with designing the V-2 rockets and bring them to Russia and America, in effect giving them immunity from prosecution for war crimes. One of these Nazi scientists, Wernher von Braun, was instrumental in the development of V-2 rockets for the Nazis, and he was brought to America by the Truman Administration. Von Braun became more important than any American in the development of American rockets. In the 1950s he helped design the Jupiter class of rockets. When the United States fell behind the Soviets in the Space Race, they relied more heavily on von Braun's designs. When Apollo 11 lifted off into space, it was riding atop a Saturn V rocket designed by von Braun.

Von Braun

With the end of the war, American and Soviet scientists gained access to the plans and specifications of the German V-2 rocket. The two sides now had their hands on important, sensitive research, made all the more necessary due to the fact that their technology was well behind the Nazis' at the end of the war.

Even before the war, American scientists were experimenting with rocketry. Unlike the Germans, however, the Americans were unable to create a rocket that propelled into outer space. Regardless, the nation's scientists were actually the first to create a liquid-fueled rocket in Auburn, Massachusetts, in 1926. Four years later, the American Interplanetary Society was created in New York City, to promote the study of space travel.

Throughout the war, however, neither the Americans nor the Soviets were able to match the power of German ingenuity when it came to space exploration. With the war's end, the Americans and the Soviets seized the V-2 rocket components and specifications, sending them home to their respective laboratories for additional study. The United States harnessed the intellectual might of nearly 700 German scientists through Truman's top secret "Operation Paperclip", which stealthily relocated the scientists into America.

While the U.S. successfully brought in Nazi scientists, the proximity of Germany to Russia helped ensure it would be the Soviet Union that took much of the Nazi infrastructure left behind. Because the Soviets occupied East Germany, where much of the V-2 program was developed, it was able to capture and utilize the rocketry facilities. Quietly, the two nations began a race into space, using German advances as a springboard.

With these German resources in hand, both the Americans and the Soviets were able to project their own rockets into outer space within just a few years. Although Sputnik 1 will forever be celebrated as the first satellite to orbit Earth, America beat the Soviets in the race to project *something* into space. On March 22nd, 1946, the United States became the second nation in the world to propel an object into outer space when it successfully launched an exact replica of a German V-2 rocket outside of the earth's atmosphere. Later that year, the U.S. attached a motion picture camera to a V-2 and was able to take the first photographs and videos of the Earth from outer space. In 1947, the U.S. made great advances in using rocketry to transport living beings into space when in launched fruit flies into space aboard a V-2 rocket. Though they were just flies, this marked the first time a living organism travelled outside the earth's atmosphere.

Across the world, the Soviets were not so quick to enter space. The U.S. had the benefit not only of German scientists, but also of having German V-2 rockets on hand. It was thus much easier to copy the V-2 in America than in the Soviet Union, which only had specifications, blueprints and building materials. During the rest of the 1940s, the Soviets were playing catch-up on a variety of fronts, including the space and arms races. While the U.S. had detonated a nuclear bomb in 1945, the Soviets were not able to achieve that milestone until 1949, and while the U.S. now had a workable ballistic missile in the V-2, the Soviets would not have their own until the mid-1950s. Across the Soviet sphere, there was an intellectual disdain for space travel, which was considered impractical and irrelevant to the aims of the country, but space technology was vital for reaching military superiority or at least military equality with America.

Nuclear Weapons

When Stalin was first informed by the other Allied leaders about the existence of a new secret weapon, the atomic bomb, he had to feign surprise and ignorance about it. In fact, Stalin's regime had been working on a nuclear weapons program since 1942, relying greatly upon successful Soviet espionage to help lead the way. With intelligence sources connected to the Manhattan Project, Stalin was able to keep abreast of the Allies' progress toward creating an atomic bomb. By 1945, the Soviets already had a working blueprint of America's first atomic bombs.

On August 29, 1949, the Soviets successfully tested an atomic bomb, and with that, the Soviet Union became the second nation after the U.S. to develop and possess nuclear weapons.

The first Soviet test of an atomic weapon

In early 1951, the United States established "Project MX-1593", a top secret and heavily funded program that became part of the U.S. Air Force. The purpose of MX-1593 was to create an intercontinental ballistic missile capable of carrying a nuclear warhead. The aim was, obviously, to establish a system allowing the U.S. to target a Soviet site anywhere in the world remotely.

With Project MX-1593, America seemed to hold the advantage in creating an ICBM, and von Braun had been part of the Nazi team that envisioned rockets that could bomb the East Coast of the United States itself, which would have required an intercontinental ballistic missile (ICBM). However, the Germans were unable to achieve this goal. Since von Braun had already begun the research for an ICBM, the Americans seemed positioned to make enormous progress.

However, it was the Soviets who were first to create an ICBM. On August 21st, 1957, the Soviets launched the R-7 Semyorka, which was the world's first intercontinental ballistic missile. Work on the project began in 1953, while the American program had begun two years prior, but the Soviets were nonetheless able to complete the mission earlier. The first successful test launch in 1957 allowed the missile to travel nearly 4,000 miles.

Soviet eagerness to develop an ICBM was fueled in part by the superiority of the U.S. Air Force, which was larger and more advanced than the Soviet arsenal. Thus, the USSR felt it needed alternative ways to deliver nuclear warheads into American territory if its nuclear arsenal were to remain strategically relevant and military equity or superiority was to be achieved. The creation of the ICBM essentially negated the superiority of the U.S. Air Force, erasing all strategic edges the U.S. held over the USSR. At the same time, with this success, the Soviets opened nearly a decade of dominance of space exploration, which culminated in the launching of the world's first human being into outer space.

Chapter 22: Churchill Runs Out of Time

For a man who was Leader of His Majesty's Loyal Opposition, Churchill was absent from Parliament a great deal of the time. He was, as always, interested in global affairs and this, as well as his writing, distracted him to a degree. In March 1946 he gave his famous Fulton lecture in the USA, popularizing (though not originating) the term "Iron Curtain". His warnings about the Soviet Union had huge resonance because he had, after all, been right about Germany.

In Europe he spoke at Zurich the same year, advocating closer European cooperation and a European army. He was active in those early discussions about European unity, invited to chair the Hague Conference in 1948, and seen as something of a visionary. Ultimately Churchill was to advocate a powerful, united Europe without Britain's core membership, although at the beginning of this period he did seem to contemplate a more continental role. He had come down on the side of Britain spanning the Atlantic - a political, military and cultural bridge between the USA and continental Europe. Although highly debatable, this is a view which still has much currency in modern Britain.

Domestically, he developed a powerful critique of the centralizing and statist tendencies of the Labour Government, even though by 1947 his own party had accepted the mixed economy. This was more mature than the simplistic attacks he had made during the election of 1945. Britain was to endure austerity and in 1950, war in Korea. His wife had wisely pointed out, and he ultimately accepted, that he was probably better off in opposition under such circumstances.

His brother Jack died in 1947. They had always been close, and Jack and his family had lived in Downing Street for much of the war, after their own home had been destroyed in an air raid. Yet the same year he warmed to Christopher Soames, who had married his daughter Mary and lived close to Chartwell. Soames, who won election to the House of Commons in 1950, would become a loyal political ally during Churchill's twilight years.

Attlee called an election in early 1950, after five years of exhausting and radical Labour Government. This time Churchill was fully engaged, involving himself in the preparation of a well balanced manifesto. The result was close: Attlee's majority was shaved to five seats. Churchill was Time magazine "Man of the Year"; but he was not Prime Minister.

As the country reeled from one economic crisis to another, Attlee called a second election. On 26th October, Winston Churchill went to see the King and was invited to form a Conservative government with a majority of seventeen. Many of the faces, such as Anthony Eden, were those from the war, as were most of the personal advisors. But Churchill was capable of surprising colleagues and he appointed Florence Horsbrugh as Minister of Education - Britain's first woman minister.

His style as Prime Minister however, was to be very low key. Gone were the "Action This Day" memoranda, and the attention to detail. He was 77 years old and his health was failing. He seemed out of his depth - especially with economic issues. He had an appetite only for global matters. He sought a legacy, the resolution of the rapidly escalating Cold War, and he sought it through the Anglo-American axis. In January 1952 he travelled to Washington to meet Truman. There was warmth and hospitality, but a sense that events had moved beyond Churchill, and perhaps, Britain. He was also interested, despite the pragmatic protestations of Eden, in clinging onto the naval base at Suez. When he met Eisenhower in November, it quickly became clear that there would be no U.S. support for what appeared to be imperial obsessions.

Chapter 23: Stalin's Final Years

Stalin's Death

Among the major differences between the two superpowers was their leadership. While America gained a new and fresh president every 4-8 years, Russia had been under Stalin's control for over two decades. As his health began to fail, it became apparent that he had no intention of stepping down or even looking around for a worthy successor. In fact, those who were even whispered to be interested in his position often met with bad ends. Thus, when a rumor began to go around about a plot against his life, his closest associates panicked and began to make plans to leave the country.

Around the end of 1952 and the beginning of 1953, it seemed Stalin was on the verge of conducting another purge, starting by falsifying the "Doctors' Plot", which was to accuse Jewish doctors of plotting to assassinate top Communist leaders. In addition to being obviously anti-Semitic, it has long been assumed that Stalin was going to use it as a pretext to actually purge party leaders.

As it turned out, Stalin didn't have enough time to conduct the plan. He had suffered a major heartattack in 1945 and was suffering from various other maladies by the time he had reached his mid-70s. On March 1, 1945, Stalin did not come out of his bedroom, alarming authorities who finally entered his room that night to find him lying on the floor, seemingly having suffered a stroke. When he died the next morning, the official cause of death was listed as a cerebral hemorrhage.

Since Stalin's death in early March 1953, there have been a number of conspiracy theories suggesting that he was actually murdered. Ex-Communists and other political enemies have since claimed that Stalin was poisoned by Lavrentiy Beria, who allegedly boasted that he poisoned Stalin to prevent the coming purge. Nikita Khrushchev would later recall that Beria seemed ecstatic upon finding Stalin near death on the night of March 1, even while other party leaders were too fearful to take action based on the possibility Stalin would recover and take vengeance on them. Decades later, some historians continue to speculate that Stalin was poisoned by warfarin, a powerful rat poison that causes the kind of hemorrhagic stroke he suffered.

Chapter 24: Churchill's Final Years

In June 1953 Churchill suffered a stroke at Downing Street. At the time, this was hushed up, with senior ministers stepping in and Soames running his private office. He had rallied by the time of the party conference in October, but it was obvious that he could not continue for much longer. Nonetheless, Stalin's death earlier in the year spurred him to make a final attempt at detente with Russia. He convened a conference with Eisenhower in Bermuda. Although he had won the Nobel Prize for literature that year, he would send Clementine to receive it whilst he met Eisenhower. Surprisingly, Ike sanctioned a bilateral UK-USSR meeting to explore peace options. The cabinet, alarmed at exactly what Churchill might do on his own, vetoed this final diplomatic initiative. That year he accepted the inevitable and surrendered the British base in Egypt.

Matters were drawing to a close. There seemed to be a sense of decline, both for Britain internationally, and for Churchill personally. In March 1955 he gave his last major speech in the Commons. In it, he warned of the dangers of nuclear proliferation and offered optimism for a civilized solution to the problem. Playing all sides as ever, he had commissioned Britain's own nuclear weapons program only months before.

Under increasing pressure from the Party, which needed a new leader prior to the next election, he resigned in April. Churchill was rarely seen at Westminster during those final years, although he retained his seat until 1964. He continued his writing, publishing his History of the English Speaking Peoples in four volumes, between 1956-57. Eden took office as Prime Minister and lost it in 1957, in the aftermath of the Suez crisis. Churchill claimed he would never have intervened in Suez without consulting the Americans - probably true - but nonetheless, the bullish British foreign policy towards Egypt had been his legacy to Eden, who paid the price for it.

His final years were difficult. He continued to be celebrated at home and abroad, including receiving a knighthood and honorary American citizenship, but the spark had gone. Diana committed suicide in 1964, and his relationship with Randolph, rather like the one with his own father, was difficult. Sarah Churchill became an alcoholic.

Churchill wrestled with depression, spending as much time as he could painting in the Mediterranean. Above all, he mourned for the empire and grandeur that he had imagined would outlive him. For him, Britain's decline was in a sense his own failure. On 9th January 1965 he suffered another major stroke. After two weeks in a coma, Churchill died on the 24th.

Chapter 25: The Legacies of Churchill, Stalin and Roosevelt

Roosevelt's Legacy

Franklin Delano Roosevelt is frequently ranked among the top three most influential Presidents, and for many historians he vies for the top spot with Abraham Lincoln.

FDR's Presidency rightly ranks among the most important. Few Presidents face a single crisis on the scale of the Great Depression, but no other President faced dual crises in the way Franklin Roosevelt did. Historians agree that Roosevelt handled both the economy and the war effectively, and rightly award him positive marks.

Quantifying Presidential success is easy with Franklin Roosevelt. No President except Roosevelt has ever won more than two terms in office; FDR won an astounding four terms as President of the United States. More importantly, even Roosevelt's narrowest victory in 1944 was slightly above average in both popular vote and in the electoral college. His widest margin was the greatest up to that time, and has only since been outpaced slightly by Lyndon Johnson's popular vote count in 1964. No President can even come close to competing with Roosevelt in terms of popularity while in office. Abraham Lincoln was contested, even in the North. FDR's cousin's margin of victory in 1904 was not nearly as wide as Franklin's: Teddy lost the entire South. Other great Presidents - Jefferson, Truman and Wilson – all faced electoral challenges, with Jefferson being elected only after a tie, and Truman being prematurely announced defeated in such a close election. In sum, among all US Presidents, FDR was by far and away the most successful electorally, and endures today as one of America's most popular Presidents.

Because of this enormous voter popularity, FDR was able to pass more legislation – in his first term alone – than most Presidents pass in two. The Democratic gains in the House and Senate under Roosevelt's term yielded the largest partisan margins ever in the history of the United

States Congress. The Democrats held super majorities in Congress through all of Roosevelt's first term in office. Lasting partisan strength is a significant item associated with great Presidents. After Lincoln's election, Republicans held the Presidency for all but 16 years between 1860 and 1932. Roosevelt halted this trend, and the Presidency has since been split quite evenly between Democrats and Republicans since 1932. The House and Senate, on the other hand, were controlled overwhelmingly by Democrats between 1932 and 1995, with only a few short years of Republican control in those years.

Other pieces of the Roosevelt legacy are less easy to quantify. The First and Second New Deals ushered in landmark legislation that continues to have an impact on the American economy. Most importantly, the Social Security Act, the Federal Deposit Insurance Corporation, the Securities and Exchange Commission and the Federal Communications Commission all continue to affect the fabric of American life and the nation's political debates. Other domestic legislation of a more temporary nature left an enduring impression on American society. Among these, the GI Bill allowed for the continued expansion of the US economy and the growth of the all-American suburb. Millions of Americans were catapulted into the middle class because of their service to the country in World War II. On the economy, Roosevelt's presidency was an enormous success, ending the Great Depression, and bringing unemployment from a high of 25% when he entered office to a low of less than 2% when he left. The nation went from bust to boom in just over 12 years.

On foreign policy, Roosevelt mobilized Americans effectively and won World War II, though not without some defeats along the way. Roosevelt's enormous popularity helped him to mobilize the nation in support of war, and prepared the nation for the later attack on Pearl Harbor.

Roosevelt's legacy is not without critics, however. Because Roosevelt's enormous expansion of the Federal Government is still hotly debated today, FDR is assessed differently by partisans. With the Great Recession of 2008, President Obama looked to the FDR legacy as a guide. Republicans and conservatives suggested he look elsewhere. Some historians and their GOP allies contend that the American economy did not recover because of the New Deal, but only because of the massive industrial build-up brought by the US' entry into World War II. Critics point to the "Depression within a Depression" that occurred in 1938, when unemployment actually increased from about 14% to 19% within a year. Unemployment was never able to get below 14% until 1941, when the U.S. entered the war, at which point unemployment rapidly declined much faster than it had in Roosevelt's first two terms in office, down to less than 2% by 1945.

Even on foreign policy, Roosevelt's legacy is not immune from criticism. The impending Cold War becomes crucial to assessing Roosevelt's legacy. Was Roosevelt strong enough in opposing

Soviet expansion into Eastern Europe and Asia? Some view Roosevelt's concessions to the Soviets at the final Yalta Conference as horribly unwise. The US was winning the war in Japan, and with the British freed up by an impending victory in Europe, it wasn't clear that the Soviets were needed all that much. The Manhattan Project was progressing steadily, and the US would soon have a nuclear bomb. Perhaps FDR could have limited the Soviets more effectively.

Regardless of these criticisms, there is no doubt that Franklin Roosevelt's lengthy Presidency was one of the most transformative in history, for better or for worse. The size and role of the Federal Government took on its greatest expansion in history, and became responsible for ensuring basic minimum economic guarantees to its citizens. With the end of World War II, the US was positioned as the world's most viable super power, with the Soviet Union a rapidly expanding second. The collapse of the British Empire ensured that the US would replace it as the leader of the Western free world. The United States we know today – the most powerful nation in the world – owes its origins almost directly to Franklin Roosevelt, whose political courage on the New Deal and support for military mobilization, coupled with his enormous popularity, ensured that the US was well positioned to lead the world anew.

Churchill's Legacy

Churchill's life was impressive enough without his World War II leadership; yet it is surely right that his conduct in 1940 alone merits a claim to greatness. Britain was only able to fight on because he convinced the British people that it could be done. The global implications of a British capitulation can only be imagined, thankfully.

His flaws were obvious, even during his lifetime. Old fashioned views about economics, empire, race and the rule of law led to some dreadful decisions in government and long spells in the "wilderness". His penchant for peripheral military adventures has attracted extensive criticism but needs to be considered in the context of what Britain could practically do at the time.

There is a balance sheet here, with items such as the Black and Tans and the Gold Standard on one side and others such as minimum wages and 1940 on the other. That is the political career - and Churchill was heart and soul a politician.

He was also a tremendous stylist, with the result that his speeches remain some of the most famous in the English language and his books exciting and sweeping accounts of the modern era. He never professed to be a serious historian - instead he was concerned to explain and justify his role, to explore his ideas about Anglo Saxon culture, and to entertain. All of those characteristics are the mark of a great writer, which he obviously was.

As for all of us, Churchill was driven by his own character: romantic, emotional, stubborn and brave. Of course he was an egotist, driven by his own sense of destiny. It was Keynes who, in a famous exchange with Churchill, defended himself by saying that he changed his mind when the facts changed. Actually Churchill himself would change his mind in time, and would certainly concede when he had been wrong. Indian Prime Minister Pandit Nehru received a warm welcome at Downing Street during Churchill's last premiership. He changed positions on the Gold Standard and several times, on Britain's armament policy. In 1945, driving through Berlin, he was moved and saddened by the suffering he saw, much as he had been at Omdurman nearly 50 years earlier. He bore no rancor, and the bulldog was more compassionate than most. He is easy to stereotype, less so to pin down with precision.

Towards the very end his daughter Mary asked him about possible regrets. "I should have liked my father to have lived long enough to see that I made something of my life[13]", he said.

Churchill's books remain with us, as does Churchill College Cambridge, a scientific center he established in emulation of the world renowned Massachusetts Institute of Technology. There are museums, both in the U.K. and around the world. Chartwell is open to the public, owned by the National Trust.

His name still has resonance, particularly within the modern Conservative Party. His nephew Winston Churchill served in the House of Commons during the '80s, and Mary's son Nicholas is MP for Mid Sussex, having served as a minister in John Major's government. [14] Politics seems to be indelibly marked on the family.

Perhaps author Mark Riebling put it best in his 2009 article, "Churchill's Finest Hour":

"What then is the moral of Churchill's life? He was the twentieth century's great man, but we must sharply circumscribe his greatness. Because he drew the sword from the stone in 1940, what he did before and after seems admirable. Through his steadfast stance, Churchill rallied the English to die with honor—therefore they deserved to win. Whoever shall seek to save his life shall lose it; and whoever shall lose his life shall preserve it (Luke 17:33). Yet were it not for this one courageous triumph, we might now say of him: Never had one man done so little with so much."

His life remains a huge and fascinating topic in itself, the subject of thousands of books and articles. Every reader will have his own view on Churchill's merits or otherwise - his own balance sheet. That really is the point. No matter which side readers ultimately come down upon, for anyone interested in the 20th century, Churchill refuses to be ignored.

---

[13] As told to Hastings by Mary Soames. Hastings, e book location 10060.
[14] As of May 2012, Mary is the last surviving of Sir Winston's children.

Stalin's Legacy

When Joseph Stalin died in early March of 1953, his death was greeted with more relief than sadness and more joy than grief. In 1956, Stalin's successor, Nikita Khrushchev, openly repudiated Stalin's political policies before a Congress of Communist Party leaders, declaring Stalin's reign a "violation of Leninist norms of legality". Khrushchev subsequently freed most of those whom Stalin had imprisoned, including thousands of otherwise loyal party members.

Over time, more and more was done to try to eradicate the memory of Stalin in Russia. The government pulled down statues, renamed streets and even changed the name of his beloved Stalingrad to Volgograd. The only thing they forgot was that, like Hitler, Stalin had a lot of support from his fellow countrymen during his life. While he had the blood of millions on his hands, it is doubtful that anyone in his party could dare to call their hands clean.

This monument to Stalin in Gori was destroyed in 2010

Still, the Soviets were more than content to place all the blame for the Stalinist era's excesses at the leader's feet. One Soviet book summed up the prevailing view of Stalin in the wake of his death:

> J. V. Stalin had held, since 1922, the post of General Secretary of the Communist Party Central Committee. He had made important contributions to the implementation of the Party's policy of socialist construction in the USSR, and he had won great popularity by his relentless fight against the anti-Leninist groups of the Trotskyites and Bukharinites. Since the early 1930s, however, all the successes achieved by the Soviet people in the building of socialism began to be arbitrarily attributed to Stalin. Already in a letter written back in 1922 Lenin warned the Party Central Committee: "Comrade Stalin," he wrote, "having become General Secretary, has concentrated boundless authority in his hands, and I am not sure whether he will always be able to exercise that authority with sufficient discretion." During the first few years after Lenin's death Stalin reckoned with his critical remarks. As time passed, however, he abused his position of General Secretary of the Party Central Committee more and more frequently, violating the principle of collective leadership and making independent decisions on important Party and state issues. Those personal shortcomings of which Lenin had warned manifested themselves with greater and greater insistence: his rudeness, capriciousness, intolerance of criticism, arbitrariness, excessive suspiciousness, etc. This led to unjustified restrictions of democracy, gross violations of socialist legality and repressions against prominent Party, government and military leaders and other people.

Famous Churchill Quotes

Part of what made the Bulldog so unique was his no-holds-barred style, which very famously extended to his speeches. Churchill was one of the 20th century's most quotable figures, if not its most quotable. Here are some of his more memorable lines.

"Nothing in life is so exhilarating as to be shot at without result." - *The Story of the Malakand Field Force: An Episode of Frontier War* (1898), Chapter X

The statesman who yields to war fever must realise that once the signal is given, he is no longer the master of policy but the slave of unforeseeable and uncontrollable events. – *My Early Life: A Roving Commission*, Chapter XVIII

"The era of procrastination, of half-measures, of soothing and baffling expedients, of delays, is coming to its close. In its place we are entering a period of consequences." - Speech in the House of Commons, November 12, 1936

"Britain and France had to choose between war and dishonour. They chose dishonour. They will have war." – Speech to Chamberlain after Munich

"I cannot forecast to you the action of Russia. It is a riddle wrapped in a mystery inside an enigma" – Speech, 1939

"You ask, what is our policy? I will say: It is to wage war, by sea, land and air, with all our might and with all the strength that God can give us: to wage war against a monstrous tyranny, never surpassed in the dark, lamentable catalogue of human crime. That is our policy. You ask, what is our aim? I can answer in one word: It is victory, victory at all costs, victory in spite of all terror, victory, however long and hard the road may be; for without victory, there is no survival." – Speech upon becoming PM, May 1940

"Of this I am quite sure, that if we open a quarrel between the past and the present, we shall find that we have lost the future." – Speech in June 1940

"The gratitude of every home in our Island, in our Empire, and indeed throughout the world, except in the abodes of the guilty, goes out to the British airmen who, undaunted by odds, unwearied in their constant challenge and mortal danger, are turning the tide of the World War by their prowess and by their devotion. Never in the field of human conflict was so much owed by so many to so few. All hearts go out to the fighter pilots, whose brilliant actions we see with our own eyes day after day; but we must never forget that all the time, night after night, month after month, our bomber squadrons travel far into Germany, find their targets in the darkness by the highest navigational skill, aim their attacks, often under the heaviest fire, often with serious loss, with deliberate careful discrimination, and inflict shattering blows upon the whole of the technical and war-making structure of the Nazi power." - August 1940

"We are waiting for the long-promised invasion. So are the fishes." – October, 1940

"If Hitler invaded Hell, I would make at least a favourable reference to the devil in the House of Commons." - To his personal secretary John Colville the evening before Operation Barbarossa, the German invasion of the Soviet Union.

"Hitler is a monster of wickedness, insatiable in his lust for blood and plunder. Not content with having all Europe under his heel, or else terrorised into various forms of abject submission, he must now carry his work of butchery and desolation among the vast multitudes of Russia and of Asia. The terrible military machine - which we and the rest of the civilised world so foolishly, so supinely, so insensately allowed the Nazi gangsters to build up year by year from almost nothing - cannot stand idle lest it rust or fall to pieces. ... So now this bloodthirsty guttersnipe must launch his mechanized armies upon new fields of slaughter, pillage and devastation." – June 1941

"Never give in — never, never, never, never, in nothing great or small, large or petty, never give in except to convictions of honour and good sense." – October 1941

"Now this is not the end. It is not even the beginning of the end. But it is, perhaps, the end of the beginning." – After Second El Alamein

"It seems to me that the moment has come when the question of bombing of German cities simply for the sake of increasing the terror, though under other pretexts, should be reviewed." – After the bombing of Dresden

"To achieve the extirpation of Nazi tyranny there are no lengths of violence to which we will not go." – September 1943

"The inherent vice of capitalism is the unequal sharing of blessings. The inherent virtue of Socialism is the equal sharing of miseries." – October 1945

"Meeting Roosevelt was like uncorking your first bottle of champagne." – After visiting FDR's grave.

"A shadow has fallen upon the scenes so lately lighted by the Allied victory…. From Stettin in the Baltic to Trieste in the Adriatic an iron curtain has descended across the Continent." – Speech in Missouri, 1946.

"When I was younger I made it a rule never to take strong drink before lunch. It is now my rule never to do so before breakfast." – Response to King George VI.

"Many forms of Government have been tried and will be tried in this world of sin and woe. No one pretends that democracy is perfect or all-wise. Indeed, it has been said that democracy is the worst form of government except all those other forms that have been tried from time to time." - Speech in November 1947

"War is mainly a catalogue of blunders." – From *The Second World War, Volume III : The Grand Alliance (1950)* Chapter 20 (The Soviet Nemesis)

"There is a jocular saying: 'To improve is to change; to be perfect is to have changed often.' I had to use that once or twice in my long career." – Speech before the U.S. Congress, 1952

"Dogs look up to you, cats look down on you. Give me a pig! He looks you in the eye and treats you as an equal." – Cited in *Churchill by Himself* (2008)

"An appeaser is one who feeds a crocodile — hoping it will eat him last." - *Reader's Digest* (December 1954)

"I have taken more out of alcohol than alcohol has taken out of me." - cited in *The Forbes Book of Business Quotations* (2007)

"We are all worms. But I do believe I am a glow-worm." - Quoted by Violet Bonham-Carter in *Winston Churchill as I Knew Him* (1965),

"Success is not final, failure is not fatal: it is the courage to continue that counts." – Quoted in *The Prodigal Project : Book I : Genesis* (2003)

Bibliography

Alanbrooke, Field Marshal Lord (1957) War Diaries 1939-45 (ed. Danchev, Alex and Todman, Daniel) (London: Weidenfeld and Nicolson 2001 edition).

Brinkley, Alan and Davis Dyer. *The American Presidency: The Authoritative Reference.* New York: Houghton Mifflin, 2004.

Churchill, Winston S.:

(1948-54) The Second World War (ed John Keegan, 1985) (London: Penguin 2005 edition).

(1930) My Early Life (London: Thornton Butterworth).

Gilbert, Martin (1991) Churchill: A life (London: Macmillan).

Hastings, Max (2009) Finest Years: Churchill as Warlord, 1940-45 (London: Harper Collins, 2010 e-book edition)

Holmes, Richard (2006) In the Footsteps of Churchill (London: BBC).

Jackson, Ashley (2011) Churchill (London: Quercus).

Jenkins, Roy (2000) Churchill: a biography (London: Macmillan).

Knight, Nigel (2008) Churchill: the greatest Briton unmasked (Newton Abbot: David and Charles, 2010 e-book edition)

Morgan, Ted (1982) Churchill 1874-1915 (London: Jonathan Cape).

Overy, Richard (1997) Why the Allies Won (London: Jonathan Cape).

Ponting, Clive (1990) 1940: Myth and Reality (London: Hamish Hamilton)

Reynolds, David (2004) In Command of History: Churchill fighting and writing the Second World War (London: Allen Lane).

Smith, Carter and Allen Weinstein. *Presidents: Every Question Answered.* New York: Hylas Publishing.

Stalin: The First In-depth Biography Based on Explosive New Documents from Russia's Secret Archives by Edvard Radzinskii (Paperback - Aug 18, 1997)

Stalin: The Court of the Red Tsar by Simon Sebag Montefiore (Paperback - Sep 13, 2005)

Young Stalin by Simon Sebag Montefiore (Paperback - Oct 14, 2008)

Stalin: Breaker of Nations by Robert Conquest (Paperback - Nov 1, 1992)

Stalin and His Hangmen: The Tyrant and Those Who Killed for Him by Donald Rayfield (Paperback - Dec 13, 2005)

Stalin: Russia's Man of Steel by Albert Marrin (Paperback - Jan 1, 2002)

Stalin in Power: The Revolution from Above, 1928-1941 by Robert C. Tucker (Paperback - Apr 17, 1992)

Hitler and Stalin: Parallel Lives by Alan Bullock (Paperback - Nov 2, 1993)